F P McArthur's journey is a testament to resilience and reinvention. Despite early struggles at school, he rose to become a senior aviation manager, pioneering a new division within an international airline. Later, he retrained as a therapist, dedicating himself to working with diverse individuals and organisations. As an autistic person, Finlay often finds it challenging to fit into the conventional mould—a struggle that has revealed both where he belongs and where he doesn't. In those spaces where words fail him in conversation, poetry emerges as a sanctuary, allowing him to express the emotions that define his unique perspective on life.

To my family and friends

# F P McArthur

## LINES FROM THE SOUL

Echoes of Emotion, Whispers from Life

## AUSTIN MACAULEY PUBLISHERS

LONDON * CAMBRIDGE * NEW YORK * SHARJAH

Copyright © F P McArthur 2025

The right of F P McArthur to be identified as author of this work has been asserted by the author in accordance with sections 77 and 78 of the Copyright, Designs and Patents Act 1988.

All rights reserved. No part of this publication may be reproduced, stored in a retrieval system, or transmitted in any form or by any means, electronic, mechanical, photocopying, recording, or otherwise, without the prior permission of the publishers.

Any person who commits any unauthorised act in relation to this publication may be liable to criminal prosecution and civil claims for damages.

A CIP catalogue record for this title is available from the British Library.

ISBN 9781035898770 (Paperback)
ISBN 9781035898794 (ePub e-book)
ISBN 9781035898787 (Audiobook)

www.austinmacauley.com

First Published 2025
Austin Macauley Publishers Ltd®
1 Canada Square
Canary Wharf
London
E14 5AA

To my parents, thank you for instilling in me the values of perseverance and curiosity. Your guidance and wisdom have profoundly shaped my outlook on life and have been instrumental in my personal growth. Your unwavering support has been a constant source of strength, and I am forever grateful for the foundation you provided.

To my siblings, family, and friends, thank you for being my challengers, my inspirers, and my greatest re-minders that resilience and determination matter far more than following convention. You've shown me the beauty of thinking differently and encouraged me to embrace my individuality with pride.

I am also deeply grateful for the myriad experiences life has presented me. Each challenge, triumph, and quiet moment of reflection has contributed to a broader perspective and a deeper understanding of both the world and my place within it. These lessons have taught me the value of adaptability and the importance of embracing change with an open heart and mind.

In recognising the role of my family and the transformative power of life's journey, I see how personal growth is rarely a solitary endeavour. It is through your love, support, and the lessons learnt along the way that I have been able to evolve and uncover boundless opportunities for growth and discovery.

Thank you all for being my foundation, my inspiration, and my unwavering light

To guide you through the themes and ideas woven into these verses, each section begins with a thoughtfully written article. These pieces serve as invitations—windows into the heart of the poems that follow.

The articles set the stage, offering context, insights, or musings that connect the themes of each section to our shared human experience. Whether exploring resilience, the beauty of nature, the complexities of relationships, or the depths of self-discovery, these introductions aim to enrich your reading experience and provide a lens through which to view the poems.

Poetry is deeply personal yet universally resonant. My hope is that these words, both prose and verse, create a space for reflection, inspiration, and perhaps a little discovery of your own.

So, take your time. Begin with the article, immerse yourself in the poems, and allow yourself to explore the themes in whatever way feels most meaningful to you. Thank you for joining me on this journey—one that celebrates both the power of words and the profound beauty of the human spirit.

# Table of Contents

| | |
|---|---|
| **Introduction** | 15 |
| **What Is Life** | 17 |
| **The Path Less Travelled** | 18 |
| **Navigating Life's Obstacles** | 19 |
| **Life's Mistakes** | 20 |
| **Roots of Our Resilience** | 21 |
| **I Am Only Human** | 22 |
| **Depths of My Mind** | 23 |
| **Triumph Over Tragedy** | 24 |
| **Within My Soul** | 25 |
| **Windmills of My Mind** | 26 |
| **Embrace the Journey** | 27 |
| **A Life Worth Living** | 28 |
| **Against the Odds** | 29 |
| **Surrender and Let Go** | 30 |
| **Let Dreams Take Flight** | 31 |
| **Inspire the World** | 32 |
| **Pursuit of Passion** | 33 |
| **No Regrets** | 34 |
| **Reality** | 35 |
| **Cause and Effect** | 36 |
| **In a Heartbeat of Time** | 37 |
| **Cast off the Chains** | 38 |
| **The Void** | 39 |

| | |
|---|---|
| What If | 40 |
| Feel the Presence | 41 |
| Life, My Companion | 42 |
| Solitude | 43 |
| With Every Breath | 44 |
| If I Only Had One Day Left | 45 |
| Above the Clouds | 46 |
| Another Day | 47 |
| Reach New Heights | 48 |
| Potential | 49 |
| I Yearn for Peace | 50 |
| The Importance of a Curious Mind | 51 |
| I Ascend to the Heavens | 52 |
| In the Peace of a Church | 53 |
| Yesterday's Fish and Chip Paper | 54 |
| Old Friends | 55 |
| Death Isn't Goodbye | 56 |
| In a Dream | 57 |
| What's In a Prayer | 58 |
| You Are Immortal | 59 |
| Darkness to Light | 60 |
| Ghosts in the Mist | 62 |
| Just Another Soul | 63 |
| The Stranger | 64 |
| Death of Politics | 65 |
| Through Ancient Eyes | 66 |
| Some Storms Are Positive | 67 |

| | |
|---|---|
| Time in My Hands | 68 |
| Wine | 69 |
| Sharing of Experiences to Me, Is Continuing My Learning and Growth! | 70 |
| A London Dawn | 72 |
| Ghosts of London | 74 |
| London's Heart | 76 |
| Old London Town | 78 |
| Scotland | 80 |
| The Highland Clearances | 82 |
| Wales | 84 |
| This England (Wordsworth Style) | 86 |
| New York | 88 |
| Ghosts of 9/11 | 90 |
| Time | 93 |
| Arabic Night | 95 |
| Midsummer's Eve | 97 |
| Mornings Dew | 99 |
| A Lament for the Earth | 101 |
| Rainy Woodland Walks | 103 |
| Nature's Walk | 105 |
| Sea Dreams | 107 |
| The Atlantic | 109 |
| Waves | 111 |
| Whispering Pines | 113 |
| In Tranquil Meadows | 115 |
| Eagles Cry | 117 |
| Little Oak Tree | 119 |

| | |
|---|---|
| The Holly Bush | 121 |
| On a Summer's Breeze | 123 |
| Wellbeing in Nature | 125 |
| D-Day | 127 |
| Christmas Day 1914 | 129 |
| Weinschenk 1914 | 130 |
| A Field of Poppies | 132 |
| Those Buried in Foreign Lands | 134 |
| Why War | 136 |
| A Prayer to the Fallen | 138 |
| Poems of a More Personal Nature | 139 |
| Don't Wait to Say 'I Love You' | 140 |
| Possessions | 142 |
| Chasing the Dollar | 144 |
| Private Investigation | 146 |
| The Highwayman's Code | 148 |
| Within a Desert Storm | 150 |
| An Indian Dawn | 152 |
| Ripples | 154 |
| The Secret Language of Trees | 156 |
| The Stag | 158 |
| Sunset | 160 |
| Kiss of a Rose | 162 |
| Nature's Time | 164 |
| Peace | 166 |
| In a Winter's Grip | 168 |
| Ghosts of Runnymede | 170 |

| | |
|---|---|
| By the Light of Love | 172 |
| Find the Love Within | 174 |
| In Love, We Find Peace | 176 |
| I Still Got the Blues | 178 |
| Am I Lost | 180 |
| The Old Blind Man | 182 |
| The Deaf Lady | 184 |
| The Old Lady in the Marketplace | 186 |
| The Girl on the Balcony | 188 |
| In a Woman's Tear | 190 |
| International Women's Day | 192 |
| Is My Mother Now Just a Statistic? | 194 |
| What If Love Became Extinct? | 196 |
| A Whisky Whimsy | 198 |
| The Little Girl and the Ghost | 199 |
| What If the Moon Was Made Out of Cheese? | 201 |
| The Winemaker and His Trusty Barrel | 202 |
| Ode to Tea | 204 |
| What If Trains Ran on Time? | 205 |
| Can I Really 'Catch' a Cold? | 207 |
| Time, What Time? | 208 |
| What Is Human-Kind? | 209 |
| The Old Book on the Shelf | 210 |

# Introduction

In *Lines from the Soul,* I invite you to embark on a journey through the tapestry of life as seen through my eyes. This collection draws deeply from my personal experiences of growing up with autism and my observations of the ever-changing world around us.

Within these pages, I explore themes of personal growth, resilience, nature, and the complexity of the human experience. Each poem seeks to distil the essence of emotion, thought, and connection, offering a unique perspective shaped by my own path through life.

My writing is a reflection of a life enriched by leadership, coaching, and a passion for understanding what makes us human. Blending personal introspection with universal truths and my battles with autism, these poems illuminate the power of words to heal, inspire, and forge meaningful connections.

Through the highs and lows, moments of clarity, and periods of doubt, this collection serves as a mirror of self-discovery and creative expression. My hope is that within these poems, you will find echoes of your own journey and moments that resonate with your soul.

So, join me in *Lines from the Soul* as I share this poetic voyage. Together, let us explore the beauty and depth of life's intricacies, one verse at a time.

If you ignore what you have already been told, then personal development starts.

Personal development is a journey that requires a willingness to challenge the status quo and question established norms. Often, the most profound growth comes from setting aside what you've always been told and venturing into uncharted territories of thought and action. Here's why embracing this mindset is crucial for personal development and how to cultivate it.

Conventional wisdom, while valuable, can be limiting. Societal norms, cultural expectations, and traditional beliefs shape our understanding of the world and ourselves. These influences, though often well-intentioned, can constrain our potential by fostering a narrow perspective. Personal development necessitates breaking free from these constraints to explore new possibilities and uncover authentic desires and abilities.

Ignoring what you've been told often means stepping into uncertainty. This can be intimidating, as humans naturally seek comfort and familiarity. However, personal development thrives on the edge of your comfort zone. Embracing uncertainty allows you to discover new passions, develop resilience, and cultivate a sense of adventure. It's in these uncharted waters that true growth occurs.

Personal development begins when you dare to question what you've always been told and embark on a journey of self-discovery. By challenging conventional wisdom, embracing a growth mindset, and forging your own path, you unlock the potential for profound growth and fulfilment. Remember, the journey is uniquely yours—shape it with the courage to think differently and the determination to pursue your true self.

Welcome to this collection of poems on personal development, a collection dedicated to the journey of self-discovery and transformation. Each poem within the next few pages serves as a reflection on the myriad experiences, challenges, and triumphs that shape our paths towards becoming our best selves.

# What Is Life

Life is a wisp of fleeting breath
A dance between birth and death
A journey through the winding maze
Where moments bloom and swiftly fade

Within each dawn, we should find our start
With beating hearts, we play our part
Through fields of joy and depths of woe
We learn, we grow, as we come to know

Just like rivers flowing to the sea
Our paths are traced in life and destiny
Through twists and turns, we find our way
In night's embrace and in the light of day

We strive for dreams as we chase the sun
And hope that all we seek is easily won
Yet in the peace and quiet of the night
We ponder the day and work out what's right

Life is now, but also a transient Song
A journey short, yet sometimes long
In laughter's echo, our tears may flow
Allowing our life to build and grow

Remember, life is here—don't wait in turn
Light that flame and let it brightly burn
Cherish each and every breath
Living each moment until our death.

# The Path Less Travelled

Upon this path less travelled, I set my stride
Where whispers of a life not lived softly abide
Through woods of uncertainty, I boldly roam
Seeking treasures hidden in realms unknown

The familiar track, forsaken in my wake
For I, a journey's author, my own fate I make
With courage as my compass, I chart my course
Through valleys of challenge, with unwavering force

Each step, a testament to courage I find within
Embracing the unknown, where stories begin
For on the trail less trodden, true wisdom lies
As beneath the open sky, I let my spirit fly

So, allow me to wander where few dare to tread
For in the path less travelled, my soul is fed
And though the journey be fraught with strife
I will find my way and reclaim my life.

# Navigating Life's Obstacles

Navigating life's obstacles—a relentless task
A maze of existence we try to unmask
These relentless challenges and twists of fate
Are opportunities to grow and embrace

Like an inquisitive mind, we find our way
Through life's storms, both night and day
With a steadfast heart and a determined will
We find our way and strength to fulfil

Issues may rise, strong and tall
Making us question, making us feel small
Always remember, this is not the end—
Just steps to take to make us ascend

With each trial and barrier breached
Teaches us lessons we need to preach
With resilience, courage, and wisdom gained
We navigate obstacles and troubles untamed

For within each and every challenge that's made
A new path to salvation is forged and laid
With hope in our hearts and dreams in our sight
We can navigate obstacles and walk into the light.

# Life's Mistakes

In the chaos of life, a whimsical dance
Ambitions playing out—a wicked romance
With Monday's frown and Friday's cheer
Work gets better as the weekend draws near

We can spill the coffee and make typos bloom
Always, one sock gets lost in the washing room
Raindrops giggle as they encourage puddles to play
As sunsets always blush at the end of each day

Stumbles are just jokes, lessons in disguise
It makes us chase dreams with wide-open eyes
In this comedy we call life, our minds free to roam
Laughing, always learning, finding our way home

So, make mistakes—we are just being human
Life loves a script, sometimes without reason
Pursue those hopes, make errors and blunders
Dance in the moment, don't just be a number

Then we may realise life is just a dream—
It is a stage full of players, all part of a scene
Maybe pre-written, but never pre-recorded
Always being guided, always being supported.

# Roots of Our Resilience

In the depth of our being, they lay obscured—
The roots of our resilience, steadfast, assured
Beneath the surface, where shadows reside
Slowly building strength, where hope abides.

Through stormy times and winds that wail
These roots hold firm—they will not fail
From earth, they draw life, resilience, and grace
Only in their wisdom we may find our place

When problems arrive with roaring cries
These roots of resilience will always rise
Reaching for the sky with unwavering might
Breaking out of the shackles, embracing the light

In times of despair, when the world is unkind
The roots of resilience gain strength and entwine
Weaving through adversity, forging their way—
With courage and patience, they won't ever stray

The lessons they teach are insightful and bold
They teach of the strengths we have to hold
No matter the trials and tribulations of life
They give us the stamina to take away strife

When life's storms begin to grow and assail
These roots begin to muster as they unveil
In the depths of your being, you will find the key
To weather life's chaos and set your spirit free.

# I Am Only Human

In this fragile vessel made of flesh and bone
My heart beats through a spirit grown
Through this life's joy and sorrow, I navigate
Walking in solitude within twists of fate

Upon this long and uneven path, I tread
With dreams to be realised and tears unshed
I am imperfect, with many scars left unseen
Yet pumping through my veins—a resilience so keen

Through whispering winds and silent cries
The truth is never far away—it never lies
Within laughter's dance and sorrow's song
I find my strength, yet wonder where I belong

Being human paints a canvas of emotion
Deeds of goodwill and shades of devotion
Soaring on wings of hope, banishing despair
My life—a mystery, dancing in the open air

Many mistakes have cut me bare
Some lessons learnt in the monster's lair
Yet I strive to learn and to always be
Trying to fit in—part of life's humanity

In shadows cast by this fleeting time
I am just a mortal soul, walking to a rhyme
Beneath the stars and the warming sun
Realising I am only human—my story's just begun.

# Depths of My Mind

In the depths of my mind, where shadows roam
Lays a labyrinth of thoughts, majority unknown
Where dreams take flight upon wings of rhyme
The place of my memories, most lost in time

In the quiet chambers where my fears dwell
And where hopes rise up, like a distant swell
Lies the essence of me, the person I am
A tapestry of a life, woven strand by strand

I still have doubts, those I have to navigate
Seeking the truth amidst the turmoil and heartache
I look for that spark within the darkness
That guiding light, the one I need to harness

Through a maze of pathways, I wander on
Unearthing my stories, searching until dawn
For in this confusion, I find my voice
And in this chaos, I must make my choice

So, here in my thoughts, I dare to delve
To unearth the fables I must find and tell
For in the depth of my mind's huge expanse
Lies the essence of my life's truest dance.

# Triumph Over Tragedy

In the face of tragedy, where shadows loom
Let your spirit rise, don't get lost in the gloom
From the deepest despair, a phoenix takes flight
A signal of strength, to help endure the fight

Through desperation and heartache, courage will rise
With a determined soul and steely brave eyes
For victory doesn't live in the absence of pain
But in the resilience that tragedy cannot tame

In the crumbled fragments, new hopes are born
For only in adversity, new heroes are sworn
They gather the pieces of a broken dream
Creating new patterns, as yet unseen

In the aftermath of sorrow, lessons are found
Wisdom is created on hallowed ground
As each trial is endured, a new chapter begins
Of unyielding spirit, the one that wins

With scars as your badges, rise from the fall
This is a testament to life's enduring call
Strength is not measured from unbroken pride
But by the will to conquer, not from the will to hide

In the rich tapestry of life, weave with care
Then the calling of strength becomes our prayer
For in adversity, that invades our life
We create the power to deal with strife

Embrace the strength that we possess
Let it deal with life's daily worries and stress
Triumph over tragedy, let it be our decree
The let your spirit go, let it fly and be free.

# Within My Soul

Within the quiet chambers of my soul's abode
Echoes linger, whispers of stories to be told
In the depths of my mind, a universe unfolds
Where emotions dance in memories so bold

In the shadows cast by the light of self-awareness
My heart sings a melody of timeless caress
In solitude's embrace, my reflections find their way
Navigating a maze of thoughts that dance and sway

Here amidst the labyrinth of my inner rhyme
I find the essence of me, at my truest prime
As within myself, lies a universe so vast—
A tapestry of memories, of the present and past.

# Windmills of My Mind

As the corners of consciousness spin and whirl
Creating windmills in my mind, a curious swirl
These blades of imagination coil and turn
In the landscapes of dreams, where ideas burn
Catching the breeze of inspiration's flight
With quiet whispering, they dance in the night
Guided through the heavens in an endless haze
These windmills of the mind, a mystical maze
They create an orchestra, a symphony of sound
As they tune into my thoughts, distinct, profound
In the depths of my memory, so distinct and grand
They forever move forward within my mind's fertile land.

# Embrace the Journey

In a new dawn's early light
Walk an unchartered path, wild and free
Embrace the journey, just take flight—
This is your destiny, and nature's decree

Each step is one you can score
As you use courage as your guiding star
A personal story waiting to explore
To find out who you really are

Each journey has lows and highs
For it is the journey, not the end
So let your curiosity amplify
Allowing wisdom to be your friend

Accept the challenges that will come
For within every stumble, you will rise
This is just feedback from a life undone
As you soar higher, reaching for the skies

Within storms, rain, sunshine, and calm
Seize the thread of fate's design
Look at purpose etched on your palm
As life's rich tapestry starts to unwind

Accept the journey, release the strife
Caress what unfolds, be bold and true
For only in this quest, you truly find life—
The one which belongs only to you.

# A Life Worth Living

A life worth living is not measured in years
But in the joy, laughter, sorrow, and tears
In moments shared with those we hold dear
And memories cherished year after year

It's in the kindness we share, and freely give
In the strength to love, to laugh, to live
In dreams pursued with passion and zeal
The courage to talk about the love we feel

Life is worth living, even if we take a fall
It is in the beauty of nature, in heeding the call
To live authentically, being true to oneself
Finding purpose in service, in love, in health

Embrace each day, feel its present, its gift
Live with gratitude, letting our spirits uplift
For a life worth living is ours to create
In every choice we make, we relent to fate.

# Against the Odds

In our modern world of doubt and despair
In this world that's fierce and unkind
Where fear and anxiety cloak the air
Dreams are shattered, with hopes confined

Through trials and tribulations, it persists
A warrior's heart, fuelled by desire
Defying the doubters, the cynics twist
Against the odds, it climbs even higher

When dark clouds descend, casting their gloom
Where troubles rise, blocking desires
A resilient soul musters the strength to bloom
Against the odds, the flame burns brighter

In life we stumble, which is a lesson earned
The journey can be tough, as it takes a bite
Each setback is a chance to learn
Against the odds, our resilience takes flight

Through adversity's grip, it finds its way
For every slip and fall, it endures
In moments of weakness, it doesn't sway
Against the odds, it perseveres

With steely determination, as it's guiding light
Although the path may twist and bend
It weaves through darkness, shinning bright
Against the odds, it reaches the end

Remember that in times of despair
When all seems lost, and we don't believe
Our strength to endure is beyond compare
Against the odds, we find our true belief.

# Surrender and Let Go

In the quiet reframe of a darkened night
Where shadows dance in a moonlit glow
A heart once clenched in stubborn fight
Learns to surrender, learns to let go

The storms that rage within my soul
Beginning to fade into a gentle breeze
As the tides of time, that relentless roll
Bringing a welcomed, sweet release

No longer bound by chains of fear
No longer gripped by pains embrace
I sigh freedoms lament, pure and clear
And find in stillness, a sacred space

The past dissolves like a morning's dew
Beneath the warmth of a rising sun
My scars, a tale of something learnt and true
Of battles fought and victories won

To hold too tight is to banish or confine
The beauty of what's meant to be
For life is just but a fleeting line
Like a river flowing to the sea

Let the river flow and takes is course
Through valleys deep and mountains high
In yielding to its gentle force
We can touch an infinite sky

In this surrender, I am found
A soul reborn, a heart aglow
Released from every weight that bounds
As I learn to surrender and learn to let go.

# Let Dreams Take Flight

In the depths of the mind, so quiet and still
Letting your thoughts go is a crafted skill
Where your dreams take flight on wings of grace
Free to explore the realms of time and space

In the depths of mamba-black skies
Where twinkling stars look like a thousand eyes
Dreams unfurl like sails of pure delight
Guided by the pulse of hope and gentle light

Allow them to climb above this earthly fray
Ascend where doubts and fears cannot stray
Dreams are simply messages from the heart
Taking on a journey where your spirit can depart

Each dream is where new orbits are found
Cast in this endless universe, free and unbound
They create a new horizon, colourful and bright
A tapestry of love, sailing in an endless night

Be still your mind, let your dreams take flight
Taking your imagination and soul to new heights
Permit them to source magic with all their might
By inviting your creativity, love, and soul to ignite.

# Inspire the World

In the space of dreams where stars ignite
Where the tapestry of magic is spun
Is the place where hope's flame takes flight
Inspiring hearts beneath the sun

Among the darkest, shadowed night
Where words are swords and colours bold
A beacon shines, a glowing light
Forging a path, of stories to be told

Being as one, we can shine and rise above
Surrounding every soul on this great sphere
With empathy and grace, embrace the love
As we move together, we erase the fear

Allow courage to dance with grace and mirth
In every voice, a symphony of hope
Unleash the song of boundless worth
Let harmony and ambition elope

Our world of wondrous sights unseen
With brushstrokes bold and gentle hue
The canvas vast, the colours keen
We will paint a tale of old and new

In the deepest of dreams, we are free
Within words, we find strength and will
To sculpt a future, where we don't pay a fee
Inspires love, where imaginations fulfil

Let us write the tale's refrain
Inscribe it deep within our soul
A legacy which will always remain
To inspire, unite, and make us whole

The world awaits your artful plea
A flame that sets the world alight
To sparks a change, a jubilee
Simply let every word we write ignite.

# Pursuit of Passion

In the depths of dreams, where passions dwell
A flame burns brightly, wild and untamed
Of a heart ignited, new stories to tell
New passions to conquer, as yet unnamed

With each new breath, passion begins to grow
Longing to set our imaginations free
A hunger deep within our soul
Leading us forward, onto our destiny

Through trials and tribulations, we find our way
For only this time, we are truly alive
Guided by passion, our minds free to stray
Bringing new life, allowing us to thrive

Then let go of others, follow your path
Defying the whispers, which bring us low
Of doubt and fear, escaping the wrath
For passions call, we do not forgo

Dance to the tune, allow yourself to rise
So that life's journey is not in vain
Through highs and lows, we claim the prize
Shaping who we are, igniting the flame

Passions strength lies within every beat
As the journey is allowed to begin
Pushing us forward, with a rhythmic heat
Allowing our dreams to rise from within

Let is not falter, nor turn away
For in pursuit, we find our way
From the passion that ignites every day
We create our stories, don't let them stray.

# No Regrets

In life's rich tapestry, some regrets I find
Lessons of life, I try to leave behind
I move forward with hope in my heart
With each day bringing a fresh new start

Each thread is a woven lesson, forever entwined
Not for looking back, or trying to rewind
But for looking ahead, it's not out of reach
Life on earth is for us to own, and not to breach

I have some regrets, a taste of journey's craft
To learn and forgive, is all part of life's art
There are times I could have stopped and cried
The moments I tried to arrest the rising tide

No backward glances, just a forgiving heart
For moments in my being, I wasn't so smart
This period is for living, this isn't a rehearsal
We all make mistakes, just us, being natural.

# Reality

In the fabric of reality, woven tight
Threads of perception dance in the light
What's in a reality, but a shifting scene
A kaleidoscope of what could have been

For what we see, is a narrow band
Of the spectrum vast, beyond our hand
Colours unseen, dimensions unfurled
In the cosmic dance of this grand old world

Perceptions shape the world we know
Yet beneath the surface, truths may grow
For what's in a reality, but a fleeting glance
At the infinite possibilities, in life's vast expanse

In dreams and shadows, forever intertwined
In the depth and labyrinth of the human mind
What's in a reality, but a fragile veil
Where truth and illusions often assail

Question the depths, dare to explore
The mysteries hidden, behind every door
For in the heart of existence, lies the key
To unlock the secrets of what could be

What's in a reality, but a boundless sea
Of endless wonder, for you and me
So, embrace the journey, open your eyes
And discover the magic, beneath open skies.

# Cause and Effect

In the space where stars dance a cosmic ballet
Lies a tale of cause and effect, active night and day
For in every action, there is a reaction, a chain
As threads of fate are spun in life's intricate game

A whispering breeze stirs a leaf to flight
To ripples in the water, from a pebble might
Every motion, each tremor, a story unfolds
As echoes of causation in the universe are told

In the sun's warm embrace, a seed takes its stand
Roots delve deep, reaching out, part of a plan
The fertile earth stretches and grows
A testament to the virtues of life it bestows

Beware of the shadow cast by a careless hand
In the realm of cause and effect, there is no command
No act goes unanswered, no deed without consequence
A cosmic cycle unbroken, no providence

Within every word spoken, and every choice made
The tapestry of existence is endlessly laid
A delicate balance, a symphony's song
Where cause and effect meet, the dance goes on

So, heed the call of the interconnected whole
In this grand design, every part plays a role
The flowing energy of time's ceaseless stream
Where the consequence of cause and effect reigns supreme.

# In a Heartbeat of Time

In the realm where seconds softly blend
Is a heartbeat's tale, where moments wend
Time whispers and weaves through the air
Where it marches on, without a care

In each beat, a chapter of life's embrace
A symphony of moments, a dance of grace
The heartbeat, a metronome unseen
Guiding us through life, and the hours between

The tempo quickens with every moment of glee
A subtle flutter, allowing us to be wild and free
Yet, it slows with every regret, and sorrow's descent
To a sombre rhythm, playing a lowly lament

As the future beckons, with mysteries untold
Time is a heartbeat waiting to unfold
We listen to the drum, a tempo so sweet
A song of resilience, within each and every beat

So, let the heartbeat echo in the chambers of time
A poetic dance, one rhythmic and sublime
In this natural design, each beat has a part
Let this timeless melody be the music of the heart.

# Cast off the Chains

Beneath the burden of restraints unseen
A soul in bondage, with dreams redeemed
Yet within the heart, a fire still remains
Yearning to break free from binding chains

Cast off these shackles, forged in doubt
Allow courage to rise, dispel the drought
Your spirit, the phoenix—permit it to soar
And let it dance in your mind forevermore

Within this life, break the idea of conformity
Uncage your resolve, become wild and free
Release the ties that hold and bind your soul
Embrace the journey, make your spirit whole

Your chains may rattle, but fear them not
For bravery resides in the darkest plot
Shatter your limitations, embrace the unknown
In the symphony of freedom, find your tone

The past may linger, like a time-forgotten ghost
But in liberation's embrace, we make the most
Forge ahead, to where the shadows fade
Where your personality's anthem is consistently played

Cast off the chains, those which detain and bind
Let the winds of change blow; allow them to remind
You are more than what holds you, those which confine—
You're a spirit unchained, one which forever shines.

# The Void

In the depth of life, a space resides
A place between this life and the next
No words can grasp it, no words can speak it
This realm of absence, leaving science perplexed

It has no colour, nor shape to its domain
Stretching beyond what the eyes perceive
No sound can be heard, nor whispers remain—
It is a chasm of nothing, where shadows cleave

No drumbeat dances upon its veil
No warmth, no cold, no senses found
No laughter or tears to break the stale
Just a cavernous abyss, immense and profound

It calls the lost, the weary, the torn
Those seeking solace from life's cruel façade
It preys on those struggling and forlorn
Bringing a hollow embrace to those feeling flawed

Within this void, a flicker ignites—
A tiny spark, refusing to yield
Perhaps a glimmer of hope, a ray of light
Whispers of grace, or wonder revealed

It shines ever brighter, defying the dark
For even in darkness, light shows the way
This void becomes a solace, making its mark
Illuminating the path, not letting you sway

In this void, it is hope we find
Where inner strength becomes defined
A place where we leave doubt behind—
Within the void, new life is found.

# What If

What if the stars, shining bright at night
Were mere fireflies, dancing bright?
Would our dreams still reach the sky
Or would they falter, fall, and simply die?

What would happen if the sun refused to rise
And left us in darkness, hiding the sky?
Could we find our way out of the gloom
Or give up, living forever in our tomb?

What if the birds forgot to sing
And the joy they bring simply took wing?
Would we find the strength to carry on
Or fall back and dwell on what has gone?

What if the oceans ceased to flow
And tides forgot their strength and glow?
Would life still dance and play on the shore
Or wither away forevermore?

But what if hope refused to fade
And love, in darkness, found a way?
Then, in the face of all that's dire
We would find the space to ignite the fire

For what if we embrace and trust in uncertainty
Find the truth and strength of what could be
Then, in every 'what if' lies a chance
To shape our fate with bold advance.

# Feel the Presence

In the yellow hue of dawn's first light
When my world is bathed in gold
I feel my presence, pure and bright—
A mystery beginning to unfold

In the heart, where truth resides
In the souls deep, sacred dance
I feel the presence as it guides
Though the realms of fate and chance

In each breath, and in every beat
In life's continuous ebb and flow
Feel the presence of being, warm and sweet
And let its eternal grace within you grow.

# Life, My Companion

In the essence of life, I find
Time is going, leaving me behind
So many plans yet to unfold—
I have to be strong, cunning, and bold
To not let things slip away
But to live, have fun, laugh, and play
Then I can say I have prevailed and learnt
I didn't let go, I wasn't burnt
But lived a full, exciting life
Where I conquered life's troubles and strife
Then I can hold up my head and speak
"Life was my companion, each and every day."

# Solitude

In solitude's embrace, my soul finds peace
In the depths of silence, worries release
Echoes of emotion, whispers of truth
Causing the troubles of my mind to cease.

# With Every Breath

With every breath in, a new me is born
With every breath out, an old part of me dies
Each sensation I feel is temporary; nothing lasts
Every thought I have is a fleeting moment in time
I pass this way but once, as time simply unfolds
My being is part of the universe and the life it holds.

# If I Only Had One Day Left

If I only had one day left to live, how would I spend this time?
Savour each moment and make each second mine
I would meet this last day with a smile on my face
Embracing a new dawn within this fleeting, precious space

I would tell my loved ones how I truly love and care
For within this limited time, I would share this bond so rare
I would laugh, share memories, and moments so dear
Creating lasting chronicles to last year by year

Maybe I would take a walk in nature, feel the sun on my face
Smell the flowers and forest, as my heart feels nature's embrace
Then watch the clouds roll by and applaud the birds in flight
Appreciate the wonders of the world as day gives way to night

I would eat the finest foods and sip from my favourite cup—
Maybe have some wine, as I am not giving up on that
I'd play my favourite music, letting its rhythm unfold
Bathe in the musing, letting my imagination take hold

Then I would allow one more moment to reflect and ponder
To reminisce, as there won't be any point in looking yonder
I would give thanks and grace for the beauty all around
Making the most of every second on this sacred ground

If I only had one more day to live, I would live it without regret
Making every moment count on this day I would never forget
Life is but a fleeting gift, it's a treasure to behold—
Live each day like it is your last. Love, laugh, be true, and be bold.

# Above the Clouds

Above the clouds on a thoughtful night
Will I reconnect with my dreams of old?
The ones I had—what marvellous delights
The ones I didn't follow, when I wasn't so bold

Upward, beyond the confines of the earth
Is the realm untethered, where fantasises heave
In this ethereal haven, where dreams give birth
Is where my thoughts and wishes gentle weave

My visions touch the peaks that soar up high
These feathers of possibility waft in Nirvana's embrace
Beyond the unseen, in a night-blackened sky
Caressing my soul, leaving a trail of grace

Tonight, I let my dreams ascend, allowing them to ignite
My spirit escorting my thoughts on their silken, quiet flight.

# Another Day

Is tomorrow simply another day?
One similar to the dawning of today?
Or will it be altogether different
One to help us on our way?

As night descends, a question remains:
What will allow you to walk in the light?
Will there be change you hope to gain
Or will you simply give in and take flight?

What if tomorrow never comes?
All your dreams wishes become undone
Will your life beat to the sound of the drum
As you greet the warmth of a rising sun?

Or will it have all been in vain?
No future, no spark to ignite the flame
Maybe tomorrow is yours to tame
With no one but yourself to blame

Tomorrow takes a step out of the dark—
Make it count, the one that matters
Hold up your head, make your mark
The rest is not your issue; leave it in tatters

Then bid yesterday farewell and goodbye—
It has done its job, it's no longer alive
Set your sights high, reach for the sky
Then grab the possible—live and thrive.

# Reach New Heights

Reach up where dreams take flight
Within an endless sky, we reach new heights
With dreams to hold and possibilities ablaze
We stride though life's endless maze

We push ahead to a distant goal
As the path we walk feeds our soul
In every step, we will rise above
So open your heart and feel the love

Waiting for the right time makes us stray
Where we tumble and fall, losing our way
Have faith in self and in the open skies
Reach new peaks with love at your side

Through mountains high and valleys low
You will conquer fear wherever you go
For in your heart, the fire ignites
Facing challenges and reaching new heights

Be bold, be fearless, don't be bound by fate
Open your imagination—let dreams create
This will open hope where spirits soar
Then you can reach heights like never before.

# Potential

In the heart of every soul, a fire burns bright
A flame of potential, a beacon in the night
It comes alive with every breath we take
A promise of greater things, a destiny to make

In the depths of our being, it quietly resides
Waiting for the moment when it cannot be denied
It whispers of dreams and hopes yet unseen
A melody of possibilities, a future serene

All too often, we doubt; we let in anxiety and fear
We let uncertainty cloud what could be clear
Hiding from our truth, afraid to shine
Unaware that our brilliance is wholly divine

Yet within us lies a power, untamed and true
A force that can shape the world in all we do
For when we embrace our true potential's call
We break down the barriers and rise above all

So ignite that flame, let it grown and blaze high
Chase after your dreams, reach for the sky
For in each of us lies greatness, waiting to be found—
A true potential of treasures, limitless and unbound.

# I Yearn for Peace

In this life, I have often sought a tranquil shore
Yet never craved the calm as I do this hour's roar
I've journeyed long, I've travelled far and wide
But now, the yearning for peace I cannot hide

In days of yore, ambitions fire burnt bright
I chased dreams through day and endless night
But now, amidst the clamour and strife
I long for stillness for the rest of my life

For in silence, whispers of truth arise
Revealing the beauty hidden 'neath endless skies
In quiet moments, my soul finds its song
And in the hush, I've found where I belong

No more the bustle of a crowded street
No more the rush of hurried, restless feet
Give me instead the peace of a tranquil stream
Where I can rest, where I can sit and dream

I have never craved peace so much
To feel its gentle and soothing touch
In a world of chaos, let peace unfurl its wing
And in its embrace, let my heart forever sing

For in the stillness, I find my truest self
In the quiet, I discover untold wealth
So let the world spin on its endless face
For only in peace, I find my sacred space.

# The Importance of a Curious Mind

Curiosity is the spark that ignites the flame of human progress. It drives exploration, fuels innovation, and propels us towards new frontiers of knowledge and understanding. Without a curious mind, our world would be static, devoid of the advancements that have shaped our civilisation. Here's why curiosity is indispensable and how it has influenced every aspect of human life.

On a personal level, curiosity fosters lifelong learning about the world around us, including self-improvement. It encourages us to explore new interests, acquire new skills, and expand our horizons. Curiosity-driven learning leads to a more fulfilling and enriched life, as it enables us to continuously grow and adapt in an ever-changing world. Without curiosity, personal development would stagnate, and our potential would remain unfulfilled.

Curiosity is the bedrock upon which human progress is built. It is the driving force behind our quest for knowledge, innovation, and understanding. Without a curious mind, we would remain confined to the limitations of our current knowledge and capabilities. It is through curiosity that we explore new frontiers, push the boundaries of what is possible, and continuously strive for a better future. Embracing and nurturing curiosity is essential for the continued growth and advancement of individuals and society as a whole. Without it, we would indeed have nothing.

This next collection, **Curiosity and the World Around Us**, delves into the essence of human inquisitiveness and the beauty of our surroundings. Each poem in this collection is a journey—an exploration of the questions that stir our minds and the marvels that enrich our lives. I hope you enjoy.

# I Ascend to the Heavens

My flight of fantasy breaks bonds with the earth
Ascending into the heavens like a homesick angel
Dancing over the clouds, touching the void
My heart at last free, so I can just be

Above, the blue is a vast, infinite space
Below, the place where my dreams came true
Yet here, in between, I feel light and free
For the first time, I think I know me

The noise of everyday life far away
The peace of the heavens all around
I feel connected and alive, free from clutter
As I become a spirit, weightless and sky-bound

I dance with the eddies and gentle winds
I am devoid of fear and earthbound worries
Feeling sad for those left behind
But knowing one day, we will again be together

For now, I drift and flow with careless mirth
Which I haven't done since the day of my birth
I have lived a good life, but now I let go of my vision
Returning to those I love—those who remained hidden.

# In the Peace of a Church

In the moonlit peace of an ancient church
Where years of prayers and candles glow
In the softness these ancient walls betray
To the vastness of the nave where my spirit grows

Calmness surrounds me as shadows flicker
As the smell of incense catches my throat
Stained glass windows reflecting the light
Splashing colours of old throughout the year

I sit, my mind restful in this tranquil space
The odour of bygone wood and damp fills the air
My being feeling restful and serene
In this holy place, where just being is so rare

As I leave this chapel, this peace and calm
Walking back out into a turbulent world
I leave a part of my quietened heart behind
My mind finding an alliance, beginning to unfurl.

# Yesterday's Fish and Chip Paper

Fish and chips wrapped in yesterday's news
Full of facts and yesterday's views
Creating hope, confusion, and sorrow—
Here today, then gone tomorrow

All that news, of times gone by
Yesterday went in a blink of an eye
All those politics, all those debates—
Will they come true? We'll just have to wait

What is news if not just an opinion
Of some so-called expert in their dominion
Causing fear, stress, upset, and worry
Making us rush around, causing us to hurry

Then it's all change, a different story
Yesterday's big headline no longer a worry
Today, a new dawn, different things to write
Making the reader sit up and bite

Fish and chips, wrapped in yesterday's news
Vinegar and salt now distorting the views
What news has gone—would I really know
Or am I just another soul, caught up in the tow?

# Old Friends

Sitting on a park bench, watching time
Feeding the pigeons—it's not yet a crime
Overcoats done up against the cold
Reminiscing on stories never to be told

People walk past without a care
Not interested in the stories of this pair
The times of war, when they nearly died
The friends they lost, when they sat and cried

Now time is their only friend and ally
As they watch clouds drift across the sky
Years etched on their craggy faces
Remembering loved ones and sunny places

Although the seasons change, they still remain
An anchor to each other, as life shifts the terrain
Their bones aged by the passage of years
A reminder of their love that forever endears

These old friends—the treasures they are
A constant friendship that has travelled so far
Sharing life's journey as it twists and bends
Always sharing, forever caring, and unfailingly friends.

# Death Isn't Goodbye

In the future realms of light and shade
Where dreams are born and fears are laid
There dwells a spectrum, silent and sure
Whose touch we all must one day endure

Death, they call it—a distant shore
Where souls depart forevermore
But is it truly an end, a cessation
Or merely a change, a transformation?

For though we part from this earthly plane
Our spirit lingers; it never wanes
It's in the memories cherished, stories told
And in the hearts of those we leave in the cold

Fear not the distance death may pose
For in the end, it's just another prose—
An unwritten journey to somewhere yet unknown
This journey we all must make alone

But in that lowly journey, let us find
That death is but a state of mind
The love—that thread, that binds us together—
Knows no distance and connects us forever.

# In a Dream

In a dream, where imaginations play
The place where fantasies unfold in a soft array
A canvas woven from moonlight's gleam
The place where reality and illusions convene

Silken whispers spoken softly in the night
As a million stars twinkle, casting a magical sight
Through endless corridors of the unconscious mind
Dreams' enduring embrace becomes unconfined

Visions paint a canvas with hues unseen
A surreal landscape, calm and serene
Where mountains rise with timeless grace
As gentle river flows, with waves made of lace

In a scented garden, leaving time behind
Flowers bloom, liberating secrets to find
Butterflies dancing a ballet of delight
Creating delicate movements in a golden light

My visions start to grow as they come into sight
Travelling on their journey through a soft twilight
In the dance of shadows and warm moonbeams
I traverse the realms of mystery, lost in dreams

As time is suspended within this astral plane
Reality's grip begins to weaken and wane
Just allow yourself to soar on wings of love
Looking down on your life from clouds above

Fantasies become familiar, yet remain unknown
The places I have visited, others never shown
A labyrinth of thoughts, some remain untold—
Only in my dreams embrace can I truly unfold

In the morning's light flows a distant stream
Awakening me from my rightful dream
Yet buried in the echoes of a velvet night
Delicate whispers reveal a sweet respite.

# What's In a Prayer

In the hush of a mind's quiet embrace
Where peace and tranquillity find their place
A soul begins to open to a whispering plea
With the power of prayer holding the key

What's in a prayer—that gentle refrain
Where the gift of thought, bring's joy or pain
It dances on silent breath, a humbling trace
Woven in our being with a mystical grace

Within a canvas of the vast unknown
The power of prayer—this solitary tone—
Echoes resonate across mountains high
As it ascends and kisses an infinite sky

In a church of silence, devotion takes flight
A sacred communion with celestial light
What is a prayer but a yearning song
Bridging the gap where hearts belong

Prayers are not confined to temples or halls
But in our minds, where a spirit call
A concerto of words, gentle yet profound
Gathering above, in every sky and cloud

From rustling leaves to an ocean's roar
In those quiet moments we often ignore
A dialogue proclaimed in silent lines
Where quiet, soulful prayer forever shines

Let your words flow like a gentle stream
Within a cascade of wishes—a waking dream
In every prayer murmured, a universe unfurls
What's in a prayer but the heart of your world.

# You Are Immortal

Within the dance of time and space
Where stars and shadows play
Immortality—a timeless grace
A light that guides the way

Beyond the veil of flesh and bone
Where earthly forms reside
You are a spirit, free to roam
Eternal as the flow of a tide

In every heartbeat, every breath
In moments vast and small
You transcend the realms of death—
Unbound, you stand forever tall

In the silence of the soul
Where truth and beauty blend
You are immortal, true and whole—
A journey with no start or end

So, fear not the shadows cast
Nor the fading of the day
You are the future, present, past—
Free and eternal in every way.

# Darkness to Light

In the realms of darkness, where shadows creep
With timid steps, we wander and sneak
A journey begins as we navigate the dark
Treading a path into light, we leave our mark

As doubt creeps in, begins to take its toll
It is time to take these steps and let us grow
We shake off the ebony cloak that hides our soul
An ember of light means we begin to know

Through troughs, turmoil, and misty valleys
Run-down streets and tin-can alleys
Step boldly forward as shadows lose their might
Hope starts to show—a new beacon of light

When dark tries to descend, and all seems lost
Keep moving forward—don't stop at all costs
As courage becomes our friend, we forge ahead
Breaking the bonds of doubt we once fed

Don't fear the dark, for it is pointing the way—
It is a new blank canvas, allowing dreams to sway
Every step you take, the darkness retreats
In your spirit and courage, never admit defeat

As a new dawn approaches—a golden hue—
Whispers of a new life, starting anew
The sun's rays piercing the morning's gloom
The world awakens, dancing to a bold new tune

From dark to light, transformation unfolds
New stories of resilience, of the brave to be told
Against the depths of doubt, strength begins to rise
The storm clouds break, replaced by neon blue skies

Ascending from despair to the heights of delight
Allow your heart to guide you—let it take flight
In your journey, you are never alone
As love's gentle guidance will always take you home

So embrace the dark, let your spirit ignite
As within you is the grace and power to alight
From the darkness, you will always transcend—
Your life is a masterpiece, never designed to end.

# Ghosts in the Mist

In the mist which veils and cloaks the earth
The Ghosts of time walk this ancient turf
In silent whispers and shadows cast
They close around us, bringing back the past

Through the swirling grey, they silently glide
Hiding in the mist, where secrets lie
The fading echoes of lost bygone days
Veiling the truth in an ephemeral haze

These ancient spirits, lingering near
Their presence felt but never quite clear
Bringing back memories in a vaporous dance
They're caught between worlds, a spectral trance

With each step, you sense an unearthly sigh
Hidden beneath a shroud, a whispering cry
Eyes playing tricks, confused and lost
Unseen shadows, no footsteps in the frost

Movement flickers in the frozen, foggy air
Phantoms murmur tales of loss and despair—
Of love and death, of joy and pain
Forever imprinted in this colourless terrain

Through ancient forests and graveyard stones
Ghosts traverse their ethereal zones
A dance of echoes in an obtuse light
Guided by the pale moon's softest white.

# Just Another Soul

I saw her sheltering from the rain
Her mind stuck in the clouds
Her head down, face showing the strain
Keeping away from life and the crowds

The clothes she wears, in tatters
Hanging off her bony frame
I wonder what in her life matters
Keeping away from life and its games

If I offered help, would she take it
Or brush me aside, feeling lame?
She still has guts, and she has grit
Keeping away from life, feeling the shame

She hurries quickly on her way
All she owns in a plastic bag
To find shelter from this day
Keeping away from life, her hopes in rags

This poor girl, which life has let go
All she has left is her heart and soul
I doubt peace will find her and let her grow
Keeping away from life, never finding a goal

I keep her in view as she shuffles along
Her time will come; it won't take long
I deal with many humans in this state
Keeping away from life, I hum the death song

Why do humans turn on those in peril?
Why turn their back on someone in pain
Leaving them to suffer with the devil?
I just lurk in the shadows; the Grim Reaper is my name.

# The Stranger

In the shadows of a twilight, a lone figure roams
A solo form on the road, where the wild wind moans
Walking a trial beneath the moon, a silhouette in the night
A desperate, lonely journey, fuelled by a relentless plight

A new sunset paints the sky in hues of fiery red
As the journey takes him into night, no time for bed
His heart, wild and free, yet haunted by words unsaid
In the vastness of an empty dream, his focus lies ahead

Leather-worn features, chiselled from the years of strife
The stranger's spirit, like a sail, propelling him through life
Through towns, cities, and country, the stranger finds his way
Chasing down desires, as in the vast expanse, they stray

Beneath a sky of endless stars, a destiny to be revealed
The stranger moves on, hiding wounds, struggling to heal
Leaving a trail of memories, like dust in the wind
Remembering the places where shadows hide and grin

Walking through the morning, a new day softly weeps
In a world where silence is often loudest when it speaks
A heart as heavy as the moon, always yearning for the dawn
But it's in the ghostly glow of midnight where his soul is drawn

This stranger's story is forever cast and etched in the sand
A quiet, lonely ballad played by a phantom band
In the vastness of the world, where dreams collide
A lonely figure's anthem, played by many, will always abide.

# Death of Politics

In the realm of rhetoric and power's sway
The palace where politicians play games each day
Makes me ponder on politics so dire—
Once a positive system, now set on fire

Is the death of politics drawing near
As their truth and principles causes fear?
When the service to people begins to fade
It causes divides, as society becomes afraid

Once, promises spoken with passion and zeal
Now reveal an insincere, troubled appeal
Lofty words and noble, ambitious goals
Detract from the erosion of honest souls

The death of honesty is a mournful scene
Where egos clash and motives turn obscene
Amongst the chaos, lies, and endless strife
Could a glimmer of hope help to sustain life?

If politics are on the ropes, battered and bruised
Can they be reborn, if we are not confused?
It is in the hands of those who need to dare
To mend a system run by those without a care

To resurrect a spirit that's unnerved and lost
And bridge the gaps of an ideological cost
The death of politics need not be the end
But a chance of rebirth, for hearts to mend

Let us seek a brighter and truthful way
Where politics serve and doesn't stray
As before its death, there is a chance to rise
And build a system that is fair, honest, and wise.

# Through Ancient Eyes

Through ancient eyes that have gone before
We get a glimpse and tales of yore
Within their gaze, a world we explore
An abundant history, rich and pure

These eyes, these windows of the past
Where each wrinkle and line, a story cast
Holding memories which forever last
Telling of a bygone age, forever steadfast

With senescent eyes, bold and wise
Their hopes and dreams, they cannot disguise
We see an ancient earth and endless skies
In their distant gaze, their spirit resides

Sharing visions of war and dark blue skies
Trials, laughter, and heartfelt sighs
Standing tall and standing wise
Learning the laws of love, an endless prize

Through these ancient, time-riddled eyes
We find the strength to break free of ties
A legacy they leave, we will forever adore
Their footsteps cast forevermore

Let us honour those who played the game
Whose love and wisdom fanned the flame
Through enduring eyes, we find our aim
Knowing life is simply ours to tame.

# Some Storms Are Positive

Not all storms come to cause disruption
Some come to clear your path
Don't let your world give in to corruption
And bathe in others' wrath

If we take the time to understand
We find lessons where we fear to tread
Leading us to notice a wonderland
And not get lost inside our head

So, when dark clouds begin to form
Take a step back and don't lose your way
Just remember, this is not the norm
Step out of the dark and learn how to play

# Time in My Hands

Here I stand, holding time in my hands
Moments slipping away like grains of sand
Yet within its ebb and flow, I understand
Every choice I make brings a new demand

With time in my hands, I hold the key
To unlock my dreams and set them free
I need to seize the day, to make it mine
Within the dance of moments, I realign

Through joys and sorrows, I navigate
With time in my hands, I can create
A tapestry of memories, rich and grand
For in the moment, I take my stand.

# Wine

What a drink we have in wine
Being produced from age-old vines
Through ages old, their journey grows
A nectar of sweet, what pleasure shows

Within the glass, a ruby hue
Whispering tales of dreams anew
Where wine dances, swirls, and gleams
Inviting souls to find new dreams

Its fragrant nose creates a symphony
From earths embrace, a lasting melody
Each sip reveals more of the story
Of sunlit vistas and days of glory

Through ancient vines, seasons are traced
The wine's creation, part of nature's grace
Its journey mirrors life's pursuit
From tender bud to ripened fruit

So, raise a glass, let laughter begin
Friends and loved ones, let happy times sing
Of life's delights and love that guide
For in a glass of wine, new tales reside.

# Sharing of Experiences to Me, Is Continuing My Learning and Growth!

Welcome to the next collection that opens a window into the moments and memories that continue to shape my life. Each poem in this anthology is a piece of my story, a reflection of the experiences that have touched my heart and soul.

Life is a tapestry woven with threads of joy and sorrow, triumphs and challenges, dreams and realities. In these verses, I share with you the essence of my journey, capturing the emotions and insights that have emerged from the path I've walked. From the quiet moments of introspection to the vibrant episodes of adventure, each poem invites you to see the world through my eyes.

This collection is an exploration of the human experience, celebrating the connections we make, the lessons we learn, and the growth we undergo. Each poem is a testament to the resilience of the human spirit and the beauty found in both the ordinary and the extraordinary. Each poem will have a few words of introduction explaining why I wrote that particular poem.

Join me in the next part of this journey as I recount the stories that have defined me. May these poems resonate with your own experiences, offering comfort, inspiration, and a shared understanding of the complex, yet profoundly beautiful journey of life.

This first collection of poems were written during my travels and the interesting facts, history, and characters I have met along the way.

This first one was written in the autumn of 2023, when I was in London for a meeting and took an early train, which pulled into London as the dawn was breaking. I stood for a couple of minutes on Hungerford Bridge and wrote the basis of the poem below: *A London Dawn*.

# A London Dawn

In London's heart, where shadows sleep
Beneath an ashen sky, where secrets creep
Dawn breaks into life, a whispering grace
A city shaking itself from the night's embrace
As neon lights begin to dull and miss
The mighty Thames reflects this morning kiss
Shedding the void of darkness worn
Now yielding to this new day, eager, and reborn
From East to West, the sun ascends
Splashing colour, which struggles to blend
The skyline bathed in a new dawn's fire
A new canvas crafted, to create and inspire
This London dawn, where history and future meet
Creates new hopes and dreams in every walking street.

Then, on the way home, it was getting dark and it stared drizzling, which gave London an eerie atmosphere. So, on the train back home, I penned the essence of the poem below, called: *Ghosts of London.*

# Ghosts of London

In the heart of ancient London's streets
A presence is felt, unseen, untold
Places where history and whispers meet
The ghosts of London, stories of old

Around the shadowy lanes they roam
Echoes of lives, lost and found
Haunted figures struggling to get home
Within this city's history, tightly wound

In the Tower's cold, deathly embrace
A phantom step upon hallowed stone
This beheaded queen leaving her trace
Warning us of deceit, and wrongful thrones

Foggy nights bring shadows along the Thames
Of Whitechapel's secrets, forever unblessed
They groan of Jack's cruel cutting games
Leaving a spectral void that's left undressed

The theatres hold their apparitional troupe
Ghostly cheers echo throughout the night
The bards' words still find their loop
Actors of old perform with ghoulish delight

In ancient pubs where Londoners meet
Words of ancient dealings linger in the air
Their spirits linger, deceitful, forever discreet
Inviting the loafers to dream and dare

Where the ghouls of London's past reside
Let them dance through the night, forever entwined
Not scowling in corners where time collides
But showing us the present, their stories defined

When you stride through London's ancient streets
Be aware of the whispers of those before
Then listen closely, allow your heart to meet
Their legacy, and let them go forevermore

For these ghosts of London, they still will roam
They have shaped London, down to the bone
In every crevice, every historical tone
They will go on forever, as this is their home.

I have taken several trips to London over the years, and I have become more accustomed to London's heartbeat every time I go. With this in mind, the next poem was born: *London's Heart.*

# London's Heart

Amongst the noise, the fuss, and grime
There is a city that stands the test of time
A place of dreams and memories old
Where majestic stories and love unfold

In cobbled streets, shadows roam
Through whispered secrets, they find a home
Where every corner holds a tale
Of triumph, loss, where hearts set sail

The Thames, a ribbon of hope, sings its song
Through histories short and stories long
Reflecting timeworn bridges, steadfast yet true
Connecting the cities souls, both old and new

In ageless parks, where dreams find solace
Where lovers kiss, a whispered promise
The tales of present and past entwine
Where the future is bright, and forever sublime

The bustling markets and tree-lined lanes
Where solitude and beauty stand and reign
In every breath, and within every sigh
London's soul lives on, and will never die

So, when you wander, hand in hand
Through streets where history makes a stand
Walk in this city and feel your part
Forever binding yourself to London's heart

And in this final ode to London, we took a guided tour of London's hidden history, which sparked my interest in writing a poem about all the 'old' sights of London. I hope you enjoy: *Old London Town*.

# Old London Town

In old London town, where history whispers
Where time's touch has left its signature
A city of wonders, creating its own course
Creating a style of its own remorse

The Tower of London, a mighty keep
Guarding stories, within its dungeons deep
Its cobbled paths, so worn and wise
Echoing footsteps, where secrets conspire

Beneath gaslit lamps that flicker bright
Ghostly shapes, creating a symphony of the night
Shadows appear, reminding us of London's plight
As the silvery Thames slips by, a ribbon of life

From the dome of St Paul's to the bustling square
Filling the city with a vibrant air
Cries the bards, hagglers, vendors, and jesters
Blending with murmurs of ancient ancestors

The River Thames, carrying the city's dreams
A tapestry woven with life's extremes
Where imagination blooms, and talent flows
From the many bards, who write London's prose

Big Ben towers like a guardian of old
To Houses of Parliament, where passions are told
Westminster Abbey, where monarchs' stories run deep
A hallowed ground, where history can rest and sleep

Old London, a lasting empire's treasure trove
Where artefacts from every corner are woven
Remnants of its greatness, born of a global cast
Of lands and ancient cultures now long past

In a place of grandeur, where dreams unfold
The spirit of an age, and tales to behold
A vibrant opera, of sights and sounds
Old London town, forever renowned.

Now, let's move on from London, and as my name suggests, I am of Scottish heritage. It would be unfavourable of me not to write a poem about the place where my ancestors still roam, simply called: *Scotland*.

# Scotland

In a land born of legends, of deep-rooted history
Where the mists of time guard its ancient mysteries
There is a realm of rugged mountains and lochs
A place where the locals still count the costs

In a bloodied past of kings and queens
Claiming their thrones, amongst history and kin
Scotland still stands together, proud and grand
Against those who waged war against this land

The Highlands' fertility of purple and green
Heather-clad hills create a royal scene
With misty glens and mountains high
All tied together with the eagle's cry

From Glasgow's beat, a vibrant embrace
To Auld Reekie's cobbled streets, steeped in grace
Scotland's heart beats with a beguiling smile
You sense its nobility as you tread the Royal Mile

In the whisper of a Scottish breeze
The echoes of history, a timeless peace
As the bagpipes play their haunting lament
Serenading a distant warrior, whose life is spent

In a glass of whisky's golden glow
You taste the spirit of Scotland's soul
In each dram, bygone stories unfold
Of ancient tales and history, painted in gold

Caledonia, this land of ancient lore
Where tartan weaves on every shore
Your spirit fierce, your beauty rare
Forever in the hearts of the brave and fair

Let your voices sing loud and clear
Tunes on the pipes for all to hear
A land of the brave, fierce and free
Scotland's skies are open, and always will be.

Staying with Scotland for the next verse. There was a particular time when I was a wee boy, in the Highlands with my family, and learnt about a dark time in Scottish history which, for some reason, has stayed with me since. I am talking about the Highland Clearances, and how many were affected by the few. Not sure if I should have included it here, but it's my journey, so please find the next verse called: *The Highland Clearances.*

# The Highland Clearances

Within the highland glens, where freedom bloomed
Lies a tale of sorrow, of hearts forever entombed
Where the land was fertile, with spirits alive
Whence came a storm, that forever would strive

The Highland clearances, a dark cloud in time
Where the chosen ones sought riches to climb
The clan's folk, connected to this ancient soil
Were stripped from their homes, their dignity and toil

Driven from their crofts, their shelter, their history
Their lives shattered, spirits broken, by this misery
For the lairds and nobles, it was progress and domain
Make way for sheep and money, was simply their aim

Bagpipes call out, as the glens became quiet
The thriving villages emptied and silent
This land they sustained, with love and care
Now mournful, barren, for some, too much to bear

Families no longer together, as they search afar
Looking for hope, for answers in a land bearing the scars
These desolate people, hearts bearing the pain
The loss of their homes, will be forever ingrained

These are highland people, a resolve burning bright
A determination weaves within every highlander's plight
They carry their pride, their heritage lighting up the night
Never forgetting their culture, their traditions an unwavering light

In the echoes of the glens, where peace still reigns
If you listen, you hear the whispers of resilience and gains
The clearances ghosts, they will never erase
These strong highland people, with their unyielding grace.

And, as Wales is also part of my life, which does sound like a real Celtic mix, it would be rude not to write a poem about dear Wales, again simply titled *Wales*.

# Wales

In the land of rugged cliffs and ancient tales
Where the sea's salty haze forever prevails
Lies a proud land with beauty untamed
A land of legends, where dreams are made

Wales! This land of emerald green
Mountains so high, touching heavens serene
With rolling hills and valleys deep
Its age-old history makes grown men weep

Through timeless mist, castles stand proud
These memorials of the past, strong and loud
Caernarfon, Conway, and Harlech's might
Stand true and strong, guarding day and night

From Snowdon's peaks to Pembrokeshire's coast
Natures canvas, where beauty is forever engrossed
Mighty waves crash upon sacred shores
Where a bygone age is difficult to ignore

In Eisteddfod's embrace, male voices entwine
Singing ancient songs, with melodies divine
Melodic Welsh language, a symphony and grace
A vibrant, devoted culture, for all to embrace

This land of the poet, where words dance and sing
From RS Thomas to Vaughn, heartfelt verse they bring
Their words, their rhyme, are whispers carried through time
Through valleys and over mountains, their stories sublime

Cymru, your heart, your spirit cannot be confined
A flame that burns strong, fierce yet kind
A pride, a dedication, where people unite
The land of dragons, where passion takes flight.

And I have to finish with the place which I have lived in most of my life, England—a place I still believe has so much to offer and is surrounded by so much beauty and diverse landscapes and cultures.

# This England
## (Wordsworth Style)

Oh, England, cradle of the steadfast morn
Where golden meadows stretch 'neath skies adorned
With clouds that wander soft as time's own hand
Thy beauty whispers through this timeless land

From chalky cliffs that greet the endless seas
To shadowed forests stirred by ancient breeze
Thy verdant pastures hum a sacred tune
While rivers dance beneath the watchful moon

The ploughman's toil, the shepherd's call at dusk
The scent of earth, of rain, of dew, and musk
Are but thy voice, a hymn to seasons' round
In thee, the heart of life eternals found

Thy cities gleam with stories etched in stone
Each cobbled street a page, each hall a throne
The bells that chime from spires old and grand
Are echoes of a past realm we try to understand

Oh, England, where the humble hedgerow lies
Its tangled green a border 'neath wide open skies
Thy humble grace, thy steadfast roots so deep
A bond that wakes, and yet, let's spirits sleep

For though the world may rage with tempest's fight
Thy steady shores remain a beacon so bright
This England, fair and bold, a poet's muse
An endless well of beauty I will always choose.

This next one needs no real introduction and was written after a recent trip to the Big Apple, called: *New York*.

# New York

In New York City, where dreams collide
Skyscrapers reach for the stars, arms open wide
Streets alive with the hum of feet
A symphony of souls, a rhythmic beat

Central Park, an emerald in the urban sprawl
Where nature whispers and children call
A breath of fresh air admits the steel
A place where hearts can truly feel

Broadway's lights, a dazzling show
Where stars are born and legends grow
Theatres echo with applause so grand
A dreamer's stage, to a promised land

In Harlem's jazz, a soulful tune
Notes that shimmer beneath the moon
Echoes of history, rich and deep
Stories the city forever keeps

Brooklyn Bridge, a timeless span
Linking dreams to every woman and man
Over the river, a journey starts
Binding boroughs and kindred hearts

In Little Italy, aromas rise
Of pasta, wine, and old-world ties
Chinatown's streets, a burst of life
Cultures blend without worry or strife

From Wall Street's rush to Soho's flair
Fashion, finance, artistry so rare
The heartbeat of a city so deep and strong
Where everyone is free to sing their song

In the heat of New York, dreams ignite
In the hustle, the bustle, the city's lights
A mosaic of stories, each one unique
In this melting pot, all voices speak

A beacon of hope, a restless flame
Where every soul can stake their claim
The heart of New York, forever beats
In its endless, vibrant, bustling streets.

While in New York, we took a trip down to Ground Zero. The atmosphere and air are heavy with loss, and the terrible atrocity which happened there, so I was compelled to write the next poem, called: *Ghosts of 9/11*.

# Ghosts of 9/11

In the stillness of September morn
When shadows stretched long and forlorn
Whispers carried on a breeze
Echoes of a time when hearts would freeze

Twin pillars of steel reaching high
Piercing the blue, a part of the sky
Stood as symbols of might and pride
Until that day when innocence died

Smoke and fire, chaos and cries
Amidst the rubble, spirits rise
Ghosts of heroes, brave and bold
Stories of courage silently told

Their memories linger in the air
In the city's pulse, they're everywhere

Names etched in cold, hard steel
As I bow down before them and kneel
For in our hearts, they live anew
Part of us in all we do

From the ashes, we rebuild
With every tear, a hope fulfilled
For those we lost, we strive to be
A beacon of light, eternally free

In the silence of the night
When the world is bathed in moonlight
Listen closely, you might hear
The ghosts of 9/11, ever near

They whisper of love, of peace, of grace
A gentle presence, a warm embrace
Guiding us through our darkest days
With the strength of their enduring gaze

Though time moves on, and years go by
Underneath the same vast sky
Their spirits soar, their voices sing
In every autumn, in every spring

So, we remember, and we mourn
But in our hearts, new hope is born
For the ghosts of 9/11 stand
A testament to our shared land

In unity, we find our way
Honouring them, day by day
For though they're gone, they're never far
Their light, our everlasting star.

When we were at the 9/11 memorial, I couldn't believe that so many years had passed since I, like so many, watched the television with open mouths. Where had that time gone, which made me jot down a few ideas from which the next poem rose from the pages: *Time*.

# Time

In the gently flowing stream of space
Where moments dance in a silent embrace
Lies a concept both subtle and sublime
A force governing us all, the essence of time

It ebbs and flows, much like an ocean tide
With every second, creating journeys to ride
From dawn's first light to midnight's chime
It weaves a tapestry of our life's design

In the cradle of the past, memories reside
To the echoes of laughter, and tears we've cried
Fleeting as they are, like a fading rhyme
Now just memories floating in the expanse of time

The present is a gift in its transient glow
A fleeting whisper, a delicate flow
It slips through our fingers, like a rhythm divine
A priceless jewel, caught in a moment of time

It marches onwards, relentless and pure
Leaving our minds thoughtful and unsure
Through dimensions unknown, it continues to climb
A constant, eternal, universal time

So let us embrace this timeless art
With open arms and grateful hearts
For in its grasp, we learn to find
The beauty and wonder, the concept of time.

I have been working in the Middle East for many years and have built up a respect and passion for the region. One evening, I had the pleasure of sitting and enjoying an Arabian night with some local people I am friendly with, and I started writing, which the next poem is the result of.

# Arabic Night

Underneath an arid, dark night's veil
Where stars in ancient stories often sail
The moon, a bright silver crescent
Whispering timeworn secrets to the desert

Beige cool sand, a canvas for the night's display
As shadows dance beneath the palm's gentle sway
In this silent splendour, the mind is left to stray
To Bedouin stories, my imagination left to play

The warm scent of spices lingers in the air
A wafting of jasmine, their fragrance so rare
The call for prayer, a soft welcoming delight
Creating dreams, to carry through the night

These majestic lands where history is spun
Beneath an Arabic sky, these tales live on
This Arabian night, so rich and deep
In my soul, it's embraced forever I will keep.

So, for the next few poems, let's take a lighter path and let me share with you some of the verses about nature. I know I included some in my first book, but for me, nature is so important. So, as it has just gone past midsummer's night, let's start with a poem I wrote about this important time in our calendars: *Midsummer's Eve.*

# Midsummer's Eve

I cut a bloom of rose
And held it to the sky
My dreams I expose
As they ascended on high

I looked upon the moon
As it idly took its place
This special evening in June
What a beguiling, peaceful space

I struggle to speak
My words do not easily come
I cannot define what I seek
I just hear the rhythm of the drum

At last, I hear a hoary voice
A gentle reassuring tone
This night I must rejoice
On this earth we call home

This mystic land of ancient lore
Where traditions run deep
These ancient people gone before
Whose wisdom we continually seek

As midnight strikes, I sit and ponder
On what tomorrow may be
I let my mind drift and wander
As for the rest, well, that's simply up to me.

The morning after Midsummer's Eve was one heavy with dew, which inspired the next poem, simply called: *Mornings Dew*.

# Mornings Dew

The morning dew so sweet and pure
Laying a watery carpet over meadows new
Feeding life into every fibre and pour
Bringing riches, to the silver mornings hue

Kissing each flower and blade of grass
Creating sustenance for natures few
Offering all creatures hope that lasts
All enjoying this tranquil view

As the sun ascends with gentle grace
The morning dew begins to fade
Leaving the earth's tender face
As daylight spreads its golden embrace

In early light's lament, we become aware
A respect of dawn's dew, a fleeting part
Of nature's beauty, so tender and rare
Bringing life's daily, enduring restart

Let us cherish each dew-covered morn
Within its quiet reassurance, we fine our cue
As a new day begins to stir, we feel reborn
And start each day with hearts renewed

I was watching the usual rubbish that the news churns out, with its wars and political unrest, and how we must save the planet, spoken by those who have to attend at least five meetings before anyone makes a decision. So, I took myself out for a walk. Being in nature and remembering the news stories reminds me how fragile the earth is, so when I got back, the following flowed from my pen:
*A Lament for the Earth*

# A Lament for the Earth

In the gentle sloping valleys, where life used to thrive
Now make way for concrete scars, struggling to strive
Their ancient secrets, their old ways losing grace
As progress moves on, leaving a dejected trace

As we mourn nature, scarred by our hand
This once proud earth, now a sad plundered land
The echoes of an eagle's cry, replaced by a hum
Of our devious plots, that leave the landscape numb

Gone are the insects, wild flowers, and birds in decline
Replaced by footprints of civilisation, leaving nature behind
The lament of the natural world, a mournful song
We have been taking it for granted, for far too long

We should weep for nature's loss, its spirit confined
The scars run deep, but we don't seem to mind
These written words say we are running out of time
We are no longer in the solace of nature's rhyme

The loss is our world and life on this earth
The one we should love and cultivate since birth
Are we being happy to rape and pillage this land
In a way we think is right, all part of a master plan?

I often wonder what future next generations will find
When this earth is tired, and worn out of this grind
Will they see nature the way is used to be
Or will they witness the death, of the final bird and tree?

I love walking in the mornings with my little dog, and on this particular morning, it was raining hard. We took shelter, or what there was of it, in a nearby forest. Listening to the rain drip through the canopy brought the next poem to fruition: *Rainy Woodland Walks*.

# Rainy Woodland Walks

Amidst the forest's tranquilly of calm
A verdant hue, in shades of green
Raindrops fall, creating a sacred psalm
Drenching the trees in a watery sheen

Making the forest floor, dank and soft
Each droplet looking like a diamond tear
A magical sight, as raindrops waft
Making the woodland air, fresh and clear

Leaves glisten, kissed by falling rain
Earthy scents create a fragrant blend
A whispering melody, this magical domain
Creating a calm and enchanting trend

Misty tendrils, the woods embrace
As raindrops play on leaves and ferns
Dancing on woodlands gentle grace
In this mystical forest, there is much to learn

As I walk, the scene wraps me like a cloak
This special jaunt that nature gifted
Lifting my spirit, allowing senses to awake
My chance to heal, my soul uplifted

Staring at the canopy, as raindrops fall and weave
I feel alive in this watery maze
Just me, my dog amongst the magic, and the trees
How I love to be in the woodlands on rainy days.

And just in case you haven't realised how much I adore nature, here is another one: *Nature's Walk.*

# Nature's Walk

Upon the road I wander, free and alone
Beneath an arching, cerulean sky
As sunlight through the trees was thrown
Nature's secrets allow my mind to fly

I watch the clouds drift past with ease
To find the wisdom that this earth imparts
I listen to the gentle whisper of the breeze
Singing soft lullabies to ease my heart

Rustling leaves and grasses beneath my feet
As hedgerows line the path with tangled thorns
A dance of shadows, dappling light so sweet
As the blackbird's song heralds another early morn

An ancient oak, knurl branches old and wise
Stands guard, with history carved in its rings
I am in awe at this majesty, with its old, ageless eyes
And feel the teachings this old master brings

The brambles' fragrant blooms, so fair
Fill my senses in a later summer's dusk
Wildflowers and meadows perfume the air
Mixed with a woodland's damp, cooling musk

This world I walk, hidden in plain sight
In every leaf, and in every bird in flight
The beauty of the earth is a pure delight
In nature's presence, I walk and find my light

In the style of those gone before, I pause
To honour nature's love, and be free
For only in her presence, I find eternal laws
And understand the earth's deep, silent mystery.

Just in case you thought I was all about the forests, meadows, and the mountains, I also love the ocean. And recently, I had the pleasure of being on the ocean for six solid days. So, the next couple of poems are about the sea. The first of which is called: *Sea Dreams*.

# Sea Dreams

In the solace of night, where my dreams take flight
I dream of the sea, underneath a soft moon's light
A symphony of whispers, the ocean's sweet song
Reaching out to my soul, where I truly belong

I feel the salt-laced air, and breeze on my face
As I wander along the shore, in a loving embrace
The golden sands shift beneath my feet
As I dance with the surf, making me feel complete

I stare to the boundary, so straight and true
Where it meets with the heavens, a limitless view
A canvas of ambitions, and stories to be told
These untamed oceans, where secrets unfold

The seabirds are messengers, flying on high
Their cries tell of tales, each one a lullaby
I feel awaken by the rhythm of the waves
A serenade of sounds, the ones I crave

If we can hear the stories that the sea weaves
Of lost sailors, whose hearts we still grieve
As within its depths, the mysteries lie
Underneath a slate grey, mirrored sky

The moon spreads its light on the water's crest
Flirting with the waves, showing a magical quest
The stars, like diamonds, reflect in the sea
As in my dreams, my spirit flies high and free

I awake to find a new dawn breaking
So, I let go of my dreams, my nightly companion
I start a new day by checking my chart
Knowing the sea's melody sings forever in my heart.

And the second one seeks for itself, and the respect I have for all oceans, but particularly the Atlantic. So, this one is just called: *The Atlantic*.

# The Atlantic

Beneath the moon's soft, silken glow
The Atlantic's waves ebb and flow
A dance of love, both wild and free
An endless waltz upon the sea

As whispers of the ocean's sigh
Mingles with the starry sky
In each crest, we find a lover's plea
A timeless tale of life and mystery

By starlight's kiss, the waters gleam
A silvery path where lovers dream
With every swell, a sweet caress
The ocean's love in soft finesse

In the Atlantic's soul, so deep and wide
Passion and peace forever reside
A boundless love, a siren's song
The Atlantic Ocean, where hearts belong.

And something a little closer to home: from the wild Atlantic to the gentle movement of the waves lapping the seashore, I hope you enjoy: *Waves*.

# Waves

I hear the wave lapping against the shore
Taking over from the one gone before
Gripping the sand with all its might
Before letting go, as it loses the fight
This gentle ripple, soft and sincere
Is a symphony of sound, I love to hear
Soothing, caring, friendly and sure
Yet containing a power, steadfast and pure
This is simply nature at her very best
A sound so soothing it holds me to her breast
One that is caring, brave, true, and wild
Firing my imagination, so deep, so profound.

Back on dry land, where I have always found walking through a pine forest so relaxing, with the tall pines making me feel I'm walking with giants. I am lucky to have one not far from where I live, and during a recent trip, I decided to write a few lines about these wonderful trees: *Whispering Pines*.

# Whispering Pines

I hear a breeze playing amongst the pines
With ancient stories, so old and sublime
The trees bend in the presence of nature's grace
So tall and elegant, yet knowing their place

The whispering songs call in a mystical land
Beneath a darkening sky, they elegantly stand
Their needles rustling, a soft lullaby in time
This secret language, calming my busy mind

With roots searching deep into the earth
Holding firm, as they have since birth
Majestic guardians, in day and night
Cloaked in the shadows, then bathed in light

Each needle a quill in nature's hand
Writing verses upon this ancient land
A poetry of silence, a sacred tone
In this quietude, serene woodland home

Underneath a fragrant celestial dome
These pines weave tales of the unknown
A murmuring tone, peaceful and divine
In the heart of these graceful, ancient pines

If you listen closely, to their kindred soul
You will hear their tales, gently unroll
In their cooling shadow, you will find
A universe of myths, ancient and entwined.

And from pine trees, back to meadows. I love a meadow at the height of summer, well, when we get a summer that is, last year I walked through a wild meadow, with its scents and colours, which always give me a peaceful feeling, which made me write the following, which I tried to write in a more Wordsworth style: *In Tranquil Meadows.*

# In Tranquil Meadows

In a tranquil meadow, where the daisies bloom
Beneath the azure sky and golden sun
A gentle breeze dispels the morning's gloom
Whispering softly, "The day has just begun."

The larks ascend, with melodies distinct and clear
A symphony of nature filling the air
With a brooklet's sweet murmur, drawing near
Through verdant fields, their crystal waters fair

The ancient oak stands guard on the hill
Its branches wide, a haven for the thrush
Where shadows dance, and time stands still
The meadows hum in nature's gentle hush

Wildflowers paint the earth with hues divine
A tapestry of colours, rich and bright
The buttercups and clover intertwine
Creating visions of pure, simple delight

In such a place, where peace and beauty blend
The heart finds solace, free from worldly care
A meadow's charm can every soul befriend
And lift the spirit high, as light as air

Oh, meadow fair, where we freely roam
Your gentle grace still whispers in the breeze
A sanctuary, a poet's dreamlike home
Where every moment brings the heart to ease.

I have always loved eagles and what they represent, not only to me, but to the indigenous people around the world. They majesty and grace have inspired painters, poets, writers, and have become a symbol for so many things, freedom being the most important. So, this is my ode to the most majestic of birds: *Eagles Cry.*

# Eagles Cry

Gliding through a clear cobalt sky
Where ancient times and echoes lie
Outstretch wings, on eddies it roams
A subtle calling, to realms unknown

Every swoop, a dance of grace
Having trust in nature's warm embrace
From rugged peaks to valleys below
It guards the heavens for friend and foe

With a heart forever strong and free
This wild resilience, for all to see
In the wilderness, where spirits roam
Is where the eagle claims its rightful throne

This resilient raptor, untamed and high
Proclaiming its place within an open sky
A reminder that in freedom we also soar
Our spirit released, and free to explore.

Over the couple of years, I have been walking my dog near a forest where I live, and when we started walking near there, I noticed a small oak sapling trying boldly to make its way into the world. Now it has grown almost ten times its original size, so I thought, why not write something about this little tree and the pleasure it brings me seeing it grow: *Little Oak Tree.*

# Little Oak Tree

This small oak tree, fragile and bold
A courageous act, with stories to unfold
Small in stature, mighty and free
For centuries to come, this oak will just, be

From a small acorn, is where the love begun
Symbolising a loss, all part of the plan
The roots are small, but its heart is bound
Symbolising a life, that's now heavenly crowned

Through the seasons, it will grow and change
As come spring, its leaf's will rearrange
Come summer, it will offer a cool shady place
When autumn arrives, its leaves falling with grace

In winter, it holds out its branches to God
Making its shape awkward and odd
But deep within, its strength resides
A testament to time, to which it abides

This little tree, part of nature's art
A hallmark of resilience, born from the start
This tree will grow of wisdom, courage, and hue
One that is solid, dependable, steadfast, and true.

Bit of a tongue-in-cheek with this one, and while on the subject of flora and fauna, last winter, when we had a bit of snow, it always brings a smile on my face to see some holly with its carefully planned little red berries smiling bravely in the cold. So, this one is my ode to the majestic holly bush: *The Holly Bush.*

# The Holly Bush

In the soul of a winter's frosty hush
Stands the proud, yet prickly holly bush
With green leaves like polished sheen
This symbol of strength, this evergreen

Against the snow, a vibrant sight
This resilient watchman of a silent night
With berries the colour of drops of blood
A contrast against the cold, snowy flood

Standing defiant, through sun and icy gales
The holly bush thrives and never fails
A true testament to nature's plight
Standing strong through day and night

Within legends old, and tales anew
This royal shrub, a symbol forever true
A guardian of hope, in winter's clutch—
This guardian, this majesty, this holly bush.

Let's quickly warm up again with this next one, simply called: *On a Summer's Breeze.*

# On a Summer's Breeze

Beneath a pale blue summer's sky
Where meadows dressed, lounge and lie
A warm summer breeze begins to take flight
Dancing with petals, flirting and bright

The fragrance of flowers hangs in the air
Leaving traces of aromatics everywhere
Butterflies waltz in the mellow embrace
Chasing dreams in the wide-open space

In the warmth of a gentle summer's gaze
Underneath a milky yellow haze
Let the breeze weave its hearsay of old
A rhapsody of ancient tales of joy and gold.

So, thank you for reading my verses on nature, but let me finish this section with a final poem dedicated to what nature gives me, and I like to think what she may bring to all of us: *Wellbeing in Nature*.

# Wellbeing in Nature

Underneath the azure, near a tranquil lake
Wellbeing's grace, like ripples, gentle break
As a host of wildflowers softly bloom
In this solitude, my heart has endless room

Within nature, a soothing balm is found
Like a new dawn, where new dreams are crowned
The whispering breeze, a murmuring stream
Awake my soul from this tranquil dream

In the gentle depth of a twilight's sigh
Wellbeing blooms neath a moon-clad sky
Where our spirit is left to wander free
Our minds to ponder on nature's mystery

With bated breath, we dance in time
To nature's rhythm, a soothing chime
Through welkin and earth, its notes resound
Within our hearts and minds, peace is bound

Let me wander midst these scenes sublime
Where wellbeing reigns in every clime
With an open spirit, I will roam and sing
In nature's arms, my heart takes wing

So let us connected with love and strive
For wellbeing's sake, we shall prosper and thrive
In prose and verse, we find nature's design
Where our hearts and souls find peace divine.

My father was a solider in his younger days and served in the Second World War within the King's Troop Royal Artillery. These next poems are ones I have written over the years to recognise what my father did, and for those who still serve their country. As my father was involved in D-Day, it seems poignant to start with a poem about this remarkable time in history: *D-Day*.

# D-Day

June 1944 D-Day's dawn, the world holds its breath
Moments to come, etched in the halls of death
They move from sea, and the skies above
These heroes brave, with golden hearts, filled with love

They sail across the channel, in boats made of steel
Through choppy waters, to fail is not a deal
Their mission unfolds, spirts are high
To liberate Europe, gripped below a darkening sky

Into landing craft, they storm the beach
Bullets fall like rain, creating a murderous screech
Undeterred, our boys press hard ahead
This price of freedom, this gut-wrenching dread

In the skies above, fly a barrage of might
Wooden gliders, and planes take flight
Paratroopers descend, their courage so bold
To hold bridges to the rear, their bravery unfolds

Battles rage on at beach, fields, villages, and towns
Men fought for freedom, making steady ground
These poor souls fought with comrades falling
Making the scene savage, tiring, forever appalling

Worn out and jaded, they push through the line
Through guts and determination, they never resign
These comrades together, united as one
Their focused resolve, to push, till the battle is won

At the end of that day, a foothold is gained
From so many brave men, fatigued and drained
Hope begins to emerge from this fateful day
As those back home, give thanks and pray

D-Days battles, now misty through time
A testament to courage, as the eighth bell chimes
Let us never forget those who held the line
Acts of courage, of a dedication, so bold, so sublime

In these modern times, does the world not see
That only for the love for our brothers will set us free?
The songs of D-Day's heroes will go on forever
Those we must not forget, not now, not ever.

A particular time in history still fascinates me, when in 1914 allies walked across no man's land and met with German soldiers to celebrate Christmas with a game of football. A time where the horrors of war were put aside so that, 'men' could mingle and swap stories, shake hands, and simply forget for a while. This next poem is dedicated to these soldiers. The first poem is in English, the second one is in German, kindly translated into German by a family friend, Mrs Gerda Ha'erbin.

# Christmas Day 1914

Silent night
Holly night
All is calm
All is bright

Their hearts reached out
Across the desolate divide
Looking into each other's eyes
There was nowhere to hide

Hands were shaken
Smiles warmly received
In this surreal place
No hostility perceived

The swapping of humility
Laughs and good cheer
No tension in this moment
No guns to fear

A game of football
Sharing of photos
This moment of history
No hiding in the shadows

A brief encounter
Caught up in time
These brothers in arms
Standing side by side

In this moment, humanity won
On this Christmas day in 1914
A new hope rose with the rising sun
As if war itself was just a dream

This compassionate moment
When the senseless killing ceased
The pipes playing a lowly lament
Hearts briefly quiet, and briefly in peace

Round yon Virgin Mother and Child
Holy infancy so tender and mild
Sleep in heavenly peace
Sleep in heavenly… peace!

# Weinschenk 1914

Stille Nacht,
Heilig Nacht,
Alles schläft,
Easement Wacht.

Ihle Herzen fan den such,
Uber die ode Kult hinweg,
Blick ten inlander in die Augend,
Ganz hone Ver Steck

Handi warden geschüttelt,
Lachin Herzl ich emalangeni,
A diesem unwirklichen Ort
War kein Feind zu erahnen.

Demut auf beiden Seiten
‚Lachen voller Freud',
Keine Spannungen,
Waffen ruhen, weit und breit.

Ein Fußballspiel,
Fotos wurden geteilt,
Ein historischer Augenblick,
Wäre gern noch verweilt.

Eine kurze Begegnung,
In der Zeit gefangen,
Brüder an den Waffen
Seit an Seit, ohne Bangen.

Die Menschlichkeit siegte,
1914 am Weihnachtstag,
Eine neue Hoffnung erhob sich,
Als ob der Krieg nur ein Traum gewesen sein mag.

Ein Moment voller Mitgefühl,
Ohne sinnlosen Tod.
Die Pfeifen spielten eine leise Klage,
Die Herzen still und ohne Not.

Nur das traute hochheilige Paar,
Heilige Kindheit, zart und mild,
Schlaf in himmlischer Ruh,
Schlaf in himmlischer Ruh

My travels took me to Northern France, and on one occasion in the summer, I found myself overlooking the Somme. The poppies were dancing on the breeze, which inspired this next poem: *A Field of Poppies.*'

# A Field of Poppies

In ancient fields, within sheaths of gold
A crimson of poppies dance and sway
Their scarlet hue, a vibrant sight
A symbol for those who fell, far away

Petals soft, with a velvet touch
Whispering tales of love anew
A fragile beauty, admired so much
As delicate as the morning dew

Their fragrant secrets fill the air
As gentle winds whisper and caress
They lightly wave without a care
All part of their natural finesse

Each poppy accords a fleeting gem
As the seasons come and go
A symbol of life's transient stem
All part of nature's flow

Yet in their passing, they truly bestow
In hearts of those who wander near
A lasting legacy, which will forever grow
Their essence of beauty, always crystal clear

Let us cherish, and let us see
For in their brief, enchanting stay
The poppies' grace and their mystery
Teach us to embrace each and every day.

My father always talked about his mates that never came home and are buried somewhere in a corner of a foreign land. Before my father passed away, he asked me to remember them, so with this request in mind, I wrote the following; *Those Buried in Foreign Lands.*

# Those Buried in Foreign Lands

Beneath the steel and helmet's dome
A heart still beats far from home
In dug outs deep and fields of strife
These soldiers fought for a way of life

With every dawn, I hear the echoes rise
Of battles fought 'neath blood-red skies
Yet in the chaos, 'mid the fray
These soldiers' songs we still hear today

In letters penned with a trembling hand
To loved ones left in a distant land
They spoke of courage, of duty bound
Yet in each word, a prayer was found

Remember me when the night is long
Or in the whisper of a quiet song
In the rustle of the autumn leaves
And in every thought that memory weaves

For as I now lay in rank and file
I so long to see your face, your smile
To hold your hand, to feel your touch
These simple things, I will miss so much

So read these words, this humble plea
For these soldiers, we now let be
For in every sunrise, hope is reborn
In every dusk, we'll share a quiet morn

Because when the guns are silent and still
When echoes fade from vale and hill
Remember, those who gave their all
Who answered duty's solemn call.

This one I wrote at the request of a lady I knew, whose son was killed during a conflict in the early 1980s in the South Atlantic, and with her kind permission, I will share it with you now: Why War.

# Why War

Why war, we ask the silent skies
As tears fall from a mother's eyes
Why must the lands be torn asunder
By man's own hands, by iron thunder?

Why war, when words could heal the hate
When love could open every gate?
Why do we choose the path of pain
To sow the seeds of endless rain?

Why war, when children dream of light
When all they crave is a silent night?
To play in fields where peace is sown
In lands so green, where rivers flow

Why war, the question haunts our mind
A plague upon all humankind
Yet still we hope, and still we strive
For a world where all can live and thrive

So may we find the courage, strong and true
To change the course, to start anew
For in our hearts, the answer lies
To build a world where peace resides.

Finally, one to the fallen, a silent prayer to those who have given up their lives so that others may live in peace: *A Prayer to the Fallen*.

# A Prayer to the Fallen

In fields of green, where shadows lie
We honour those who fought and died
Their courage vast, their spirits high
In lasting peace, they now reside

We lift our hearts in solemn prayer
To those who rest in Heaven's care
For their sacrifice, we whisper low
In gratitude for the peace we know

These fallen souls, we speak your name
With thanks we burn an eternal flame
In memory's light, you're forever free
As we pledge to honour your memory.

# Poems of a More Personal Nature

Welcome to poems from my private collection. Each poem in this collection is a treasure, carefully curated from my private writings, and now shared with you as a testament to the emotions, thoughts, and experiences that have shaped my inner world.

This collection of poems is a mosaic of my life's most cherished and significant moments. These poems are my reflections on nature, travels, work, love, and general interests, and 'things' which I hope you will find interesting. They are the expressions of me in the form of verse, and offered to you with sincerity.

Join me and discover the beauty and complexity of the human experience as seen through my personal lens. May these poems resonate with your own feelings and experiences, and may you find solace, inspiration, and a shared sense of humanity within my words.

This first one I wrote after being at a funeral, and the husband of the lady who had passed said, 'I never said I loved her enough.' This played on my mind a little, and as such, this next poem was born from that statement: *Don't Wait to Say I Love You.*

# Don't Wait to Say 'I Love You'

In a moment's farewell, with tear-stained eyes
'I love you' escapes, a heartfelt guise
For in parting's shadow, love's truth is revealed
A bittersweet symphony, of a bond openly sealed

Why do we save true feelings to the end?
It's in the here and now, we need that special blend
Of love and hope, which takes away the pain
'I love you' should be shared now, and forever to reign

Saying 'I love you' echoes, a solace in flight
A beacon of hope, within the darkest night
Though distance may widen, and time may fly
Love's whispered promise will never die

As we say goodbye, with a heavy heart's cry
'I love you' lingers like clouds in the sky
For in the language of love's tender pain
'I love you,' just like the stars, will forever remain.

The idea for this one came from the last one, and kind of speaks for itself: *Possessions.*

# Possessions

In a world of glittering gold and gleaming jewels
Where possessions seem to dictate our worth
We're told chase after wealth's shimmer
Yet truths lie beneath the surface of the earth

For in the grand tapestry of existence
Our souls are not bound by material ties
It's not in the trinkets or jewels' persistence
But in the intangible where our true essence lies

In the end, it's not in what we own
But in how we live, and the love we sow
For possessions may fade, but the seeds we've sown
Echo through eternity, in the hearts we bestow.

There is a theme going on here, but this one I wrote when speaking to a friend who gave up his very well-paid job and bought a croft in Scotland, where he is now so happy, settled, and well. You know the rest: *Chasing the Dollar*.

# Chasing the Dollar

Chasing the dollar, a quest for riches
Ambitions soar with every stride
In the realm of money, don't burn your britches
From dusk till dawn, don't lose your pride

Stoked by desire, it makes the heart sing
Making the world's allure, a tempting embrace
Through concrete jungles, life-sucking streets
That thirst for wealth, no time to waste

The game's afoot, with a hearty beat
In boardrooms and markets, games unfold
As the dollar dances, there is no retreat
Capital gained, and lost, time to be bold

Souls of man falter, dreams are disguised
The essence of life, confused and misplaced
As the frenzy of wealth, man's last embrace
With money's gain, hearts are disgraced

This price of success is never factored
At the relentless chase, this endless race
Each dollar earned is false manufactured
As security is sought, from this fraudulent space

Chasing material gains will take their toll
In this mad frenzy, minds become a haze
This material wealth is not the goal
Beyond the dollar, is where true wealth lays

Chase the dollar, this isn't a crime
But in love, laughter, and dreams untied
Is the real chase, where we won't waste time
The true wealth, where life's riches cannot hide

In the end, when all is said and done
Let love and passion be your ultimate quest
Chasing the dollar may leave you undone
It's the love for one another that truly won.

Chasing the dollar! Which brings me onto the next one, where this time we are chasing leads and not dollars. I was always fascinated by private detectives, and after watching an old black-and-white film, it made me sit down and write this next poem, which I hope you will enjoy: *Private Detective*

# Private Investigation

In a humid, smoke-filled office
I wait for the client to arrive
With heavy, tired, overworked eyes
Earning just enough to survive

In photos, and paper trails
Finding the truth, and hidden tales
The long hours, the countless leads
I try to pacify my client's many needs

Stolen gems, a murderer's clues
A couple's secret rendezvous
In every case, I take my chance
I stay in the shadows, sneaking a glance

Solitude, my ally and friend
Sometimes these cases, never end
Truth and lies always intertwined
Sometimes the trail is hard to find

A private investigator, a heart of steel
Unlocking secrets people conceal
This darker side of human desire
Where love and passion light the pyre

In dark shady bars, and dim-lit streets
I walk a path, where darkness meets
A flickering hope, of justice's light
I am a private eye, in an endless night.

Which brings me onto another 'project' poem. Not far from where I grew up, the famous highwayman Dick (Richard) Turpin used to roam the roads back in the early 1700s. I was always captivated by his tales, which I am sure were greatly exaggerated over the years. But one book I read told of the highwayman's code. Legend has it that highwaymen ran their business with a kind of code, or kinship, which they had to abide to, and this fascinated me. So, the next 'random' verse is about a highwayman living by this code: *The Highwayman's Code.*

# The Highwayman's Code

Riding out in the shadows, cast by a moonlight's sheen
A darkened figure races, his presence daring and keen
In the code of night, a phantom's decree
A highwayman swiftly rides, his being wild and free

Through the veils of darkness, a highway unfolds
A highwayman's code, with secrets left untold
The full moon a watcher to his fate and quest
With each pounding hoofbeat, a story he invests

With a pistol by his side, a flash in his eye
A marauder's code of justice, he cannot deny
To the open road, where his destiny lies
He whispers a promise, where courage wins the prize

As the stars bear witness to this highwayman's code
Through silent landscapes, his destinies bestowed
This romantic figure sends a dreamy signal so fair
In the code of the outlaw, fate waits in its lair

This lone highwayman riding through the night
In this mystical code, binding him to the soft moonlight
A symphony of echoes, of tales to be told
In the timeless secrets of this highwayman so bold.

Heading back to nature now. I was working in Kuwait a few years ago, and in March 2011, I got caught in and witnessed the largest dust storm I have ever seen. I have been working in the Middle East for a few years, but I had never witnessed anything like this. As the storm gathered pace, I penned down the following while sitting in my hotel room, watching a rather scary orange world begin to take form: *Within a Desert Storm.*

# Within a Desert Storm

Beneath the scorching sun, where sand dunes rise
A desert storm begins to merge, mixing with arid skies
Bringing whispers of a dance, mixed with grains of gold
Within the heart of this storm, ancient stories will unfold

The near horizon blurs, as a dust cloud takes form
A symphony of sound breaks within the soul of this storm
The howling wind carries many secrets to be told
As sands begin to weave their tales, in a language of old

A sudden act of violence, as the elements collide
Within the eye of the tempest, is where old spirits abide
The palm tree and grasses seek refuge from the gale
The desert's heartbeat quickens, telling an ancient tale

Day turns to charcoal black, as the storm clouds unite
The crack of thunder punctures the desert night
Lightning joins in, illuminating the desolate plain
Giving a moment's view of a sky showing the strain

As this assault reaches a climax, performing a ballet
A passing moment in life, which will forever stay
This force of nature strides on, leaving nothing behind
No footprints in the sand, and nothing to find

As the fury retreats, the desert breathes a sign
These unforgiving ancient winds bid their final goodbye
In the vast desert planes, where old mysteries swarm
Lies the echoes of tales revealed, in a deserts storm.

Keeping on this kind of theme, when I was in India, I awoke very early one morning. I couldn't sleep for some reason, lost in time. So, I got up and took a walk down the road away from my hotel. Then, as I turned a corner, I was confronted by a dawn, which stopped me in my tracks. The colours were just incredible, and the sense of occasion washed over me. I stood for a while, watching this incredible act of nature, before returning to my hotel and passing a local market, which was just setting up to trade for the day. When I got back to my room, I sat down, and this is where the next poem was born: *An Indian Dawn*.

# An Indian Dawn

On this humid Indian morn, I begin to stir
A symphony of sounds begins to confer
The sun ascends with a golden hue
Painting the sky in shades of blue

Dust motes dance in the amber light
A ballet of particles, a mesmerising sight
The stillness broken by a calming breeze
Carrying secrets through time-worn Banyan trees

As the saffron-coloured sunbeams play
The scent of jasmine dances in the haze
Dew-kissed petals unfold with delicate grace
As nature awakes in this enchanting place

The vibrant markets begin to sway
With spices and threads giving an exotic display
Traders call out their wares with pride
In this tireless world, where cultures collide

As the dawn unfolds, sacred waters ebb and flow
Whispers of mist kiss the water's gilded glow
Morning melodies hum with nature's choir
As ancient rivers weave dreams of pure desire

On this delicate morning, India awakes
In every corner, life begins and pulsates
A melody of sights and sounds untold
In India's heart, I feel free and bold.

Staying with nature brings me to the next poem. Early one morning, taking a walk with my dog, I passed a local pond. The water was so still, just like a mirror. Being a kid at heart, I couldn't help picking up a pebble and throwing it into the water. I watched the ripples spread out from where the pebble had entered the water, which gave me the idea for this next one: *Ripples*.

# Ripples

Ripples on a pond in a dawn's embrace
Where peace and tranquillity find their space
Intricate patterns caused by the cast of a stone
As the ripples glide, creating a gentle tone

Crafting an emotive dance upon the blue
A fleeting moment, each ripple born anew
With a tender touch, they play with light
As each ripple grows larger in flight

Each wavelet whispers secrets of old
Tales of my dreams yet to unfold
A ripple's journey is brief yet grand
As it caresses and kisses the waiting land

Each movement is but a moment in time
A symphony of nature's own, in perfect rhyme
Connecting me in a silent bond
To the rhythm of life, and the great beyond.

Staying a bit longer with nature, this next poem I wrote when I was a very young boy. It's about an ancient forest my family and I visited for walks on a Sunday mornings in Surrey, where we played amongst the trees and engaged in all sorts of games. When I got home, I was inspired to write the following: *The Secret Language of Trees.*

# The Secret Language of Trees

In a green oasis, where shadows play
And sunlight dances through a leafy maze
There lies a realm where time holds no sway
Where nature sings in its mysterious way

In whispering tongues, the trees converse
Their branches swaying to a hidden tune
A language as old and wise as the universe
Echoing beneath a crescent moon

They tell of ages past, of ancient lore
Of tales etched in the bark's deep lines
Each leaf a page, telling tales from its core
Inscribed with secrets of bygone times

In every brook, an ancient story is spun
Of nature passing, seasons turning
Of battles fought and victories won
In the depths of forests, forever yearning

If we could decipher nature's cryptic speech
To grasp the essence of its silent plea
In the secret language of the tress, we reach
A communication with all that is wild and free

So, let us wander 'neath the woodland's shade
Heed the whispers that the trees bestow
For in their secret language, truth is laid
In their whispers soft, we understand and grow.

I have always found a romantic favour with the creatures of the forest, and none more than the deer that reside there. They always carry a mystic meaning for me—the way they move and interact with their surroundings. So, having recently seen a young stag in a woodland park, I wrote this next verse: *The Stag*.

# The Stag

He moves out from the shadows
Away from the forest fence
A dark brown, steely-eyed flash
His run hard and intense

Antlers reaching out to the sky
Head held high, bellowing as he moves
Into the haze of an early morning dawn
The ground shakes to thundering hooves

This natural protector, so proud and true
Stands so regal, so arrogant and tall
He commands respect from all he meets
As his hinds gather, answering his call

He is free to roam through forest and glen
Being a symbol of freedom untamed and wild
His presence stirs the hearts of men
His spirit being unrestrained and beguiled

The stag, a symbol of ancient lore
Who embodies strength, dignity, and might
A noble creature revered forevermore
One who embraces nature's eternal fight

Honour the stag's power, nobility, and grace
Its reminders us to be fearless and free
Embrace nature in this earthly space
Cherish the spirit of the stag, and just be!

Who doesn't like a sunset? This one I witnessed a few years ago while on holiday in Devon: *Sunset*.

# Sunset

As twilight's palette stains the sky's vast dome
The sun descends, giving up its right to roam
Its golden rays, like fingers, gently trace
The edges of the world with a soft embrace.

The heavens blush in shades of crimson fire
As dusk begins to show its sweet desire
A symphony of colours paints the air
As the night's grip whispers a silent prayer

The earth goes quiet in hushed anticipation
Greeting the night with deep appreciation
In whispered tones, the birds bid the day goodnight
As the stars begin to show—a celestial delight

The sunset nurtures an enduring masterpiece
A fleeting moment, yet a timeless lease
As a sunset unfolds, the world finds solace sweet
Day and night meeting in harmony, making nature complete.

My dad, when he was alive, loved his roses. We had several rose bushes and trees around the house. He would tend and nurture these wonderful plants, and in the summertime, the scent from these bushes was amazing. The neighbours were always commenting on his skill in bringing these multicoloured marvels to life, often winning prizes at local garden shows. I was talking with him as he was tending one of these little rose trees, which gave me the idea for this next one: *Kiss of a Rose*.

# Kiss of a Rose

Beneath the whispering winds of a dusky eve
Where shadows dance and twilight weaves
The kiss of a rose, so tender and deep
In the garden of dreams where secrets sleep

Petals of crimson, with a velvet embrace
A soft fragrance lingers in time and space
A kiss so pure, like the first breath of morn
In a world where love and sorrow are born

O tender rose, with your blush of fire
Awakened by the sun's desire
Your kiss—a promise of passion's bloom
A beacon of life in the gathering gloom

Beneath the moon's watchful, silvery eye
Where stars, like diamonds, shyly lie
The kiss of a rose, in the night's soft hue
A symphony of red, a lover's adieu

In the shadows of time, where memories gleam
The kiss of a rose—a whispered dream
A moment eternal in love's sweet thrall
In the heart of the night, where echoes call

The kiss of a rose, so gentle, so wild
With the innocence of a dreaming child
In the garden of whispers, where love is sown
Within your presence, a garden becomes a home.

Where do you go to fine peace, a place where you can sneak off for a while? Mine is always nature—just being outdoors, away from the hustle and bustle of life. This led me to write the following: *Nature's Time.*

# Nature's Time

As I wander beneath the open skies so vast
My heart's soft rhythm beats its cast
I walk in meadows green, where wildflowers sway
And cerebrate life's wonders in the light of day

At the entrance of a mighty forest, I stand
Feeling an interval's pulse, like grains of sand
The rustling of leaves—a lulling sound sublime—
Echoing the accent of this fleeting time

In ancient landscapes, timeless and grand
Where the past and future walk hand in hand
Is a heartbeat of time, where I find my muse
A wisdom of life—a dream in nature's hues

In the quiet and serenity of a moonlit night
A heartbeat persists—an eternal flight
A rhythmic reminder of nature's endearing art
Where a spiritual beat is etched in every heart.

Speaking of peace and quiet, I worked in London for a few years. One winter evening, I got off the train close to where I live, far removed from London's bustling streets. As I walked home, the idea for the next poem popped into my mind, simply called: *Peace*.

# **Peace**

Beneath the quilted cover of twilight's grace
In the quiet of an evening's warm embrace
A solitude of silence, as soft as a woollen fleece
Lies a sanctuary of quiet, calm, and peace

Whispers of tranquillity caress the air
Melting my heart with a tender care
My world, in response, gives a gentle release
A cloak of serenity, a soulful peace

In a magical moonlight, soft and sheen
The world bathes in a mystical dream
Diamond-like stars hold a celestial key
Unlocking my mind so it can rest and be

Time slows its dance, creating a gentle retreat
As my soul finds its place within this quiet seat
With no need to rush, it allows my mind to ease
A refuge embraced by this soulful peace

I hear the gentle rustling of leaves, a gentle sigh
Natures signing to me, a soothing lullaby
A sound of stillness, a harmonious lease
Letting my spirit fly in an endearing peace

In the present moment, I try to find
A balm for my soul, a lasting bind
With each breath, my anxieties cease
Immersed in the embrace of soulful peace.

Which season do you like? Mine is spring—and maybe autumn as well—with its colours and preparation for winter. But I do like a cold, snowy winter's day. It takes me back to when I was a small boy, where winters were cold and we had snow at least two or three times a year. We would go out and play, so with this in mind, I hope you enjoy the following: *In a Winter's Grip*.

# In a Winter's Grip

Within a winter's grip, in a cold, frosty air
A snowflake dances, beyond compare
Trees looking petrified, covered in icy lace
Sharing secrets only they can embrace

Snowmen are built, with a carrot for a nose
Wild birds puff out in a warm, cosy pose
Animals scamper, gone in a blink
As hot chocolate warms me—a luxurious drink

The ground is covered in diamonds white
The world is transformed, looking clean and bright
Footprints give away our frosty dance
And where I slipped, taking a comical chance

Coats and gloves keep us warm and snug
Having a snowball fight, then making up with a hug
Our laughter echoes in this pure and bright
In this cold winter land, this silent night

So take a chance, be brave, caress the cold
Embrace the stories wintertime unfolds
For in the midst of an icy day's chill
Warmth in fun and laughter will always fulfil.

This next one was written after a recent visit to Runnymede, where the signing of the Magna Carta took place. It is near where I grew up, and I was always fascinated with such a momentous moment in English history took place just a few miles from where I lived. This recent visit was in early autumn, and a slight mist was rising from the river, giving the place a ghostly atmosphere, which gave me the idea for this next poem: *Ghosts of Runnymede.*

# Ghosts of Runnymede

In Runnymede's historic meadows green
Where Magna Carta's echoes ring
Is the place where kings set a future scene
Sowing the seeds of England's early spring

Amidst the whispers, beside a misty river
Are the chairs of jurors, with knowledge so bold
As past and present merge and gently quiver
With reverence, to honour those who strove

Their spirit hangs in the tranquil, hazy air
In this place where history is written and flows
A gentle reminder of times so great yet rare
As the ghosts of justice forever reside and grow.

Okay, time to get a little soppy, I'm afraid! The next couple of poems look at the different aspects of love. This first one is called: *By the Light of Love.*

# By the Light of Love

By the light of love, our hearts gleam
In night's embrace, a tender dream
Where shadows dance and whispers play
In passion's realm, we find our way

The moon—a witness to our vow
As soft as silk on a lover's brow
With every sign, our spirits rise
A symphony beneath a twilight sky

By the light of love, our souls entwine
A bond eternal—so bright, so divine
In every heartbeat and every breath
We conquer life, we conquer death

Thus, in the dark, we find our flame
An endless fire for us to tame
By the light of love, we are free
To discover compassion and simply be.

Carrying on the theme of love, this next one was written after a conversation with a client who had just been through a very traumatic experience and was struggling to find a way forward in her life. During the conversation, she mentioned that the only way to move on was to find the love within herself, which she thought she had lost. After she left, it made me ponder this thought, and thus the following was written: *Find the Love Within*.

# Find the Love Within

In the quiet of your heart
Where whispers softly blend
Find the love that won't depart
A love that has no end

In the mirror of your soul
Reflecting light so true
Find the love that makes you whole
A love that's always you

Within shadows and the light
Where dreams and fears entwine
Find the love that burns so bright
A beacon that's divine

In each breath—so soft and deep
In every rise and fall
Find the love that only you can keep
The greatest love of all

In the truth that you reveal
The person you've always been
Find the love that's strong and real
And let it forever bloom within.

Staying with the theme of love, this next one is a blend of nature and love, and how they intertwine: *In Love, We Find Peace*.

# In Love, We Find Peace

Amidst the verdant hills and vales so fair
Where dappled sunlight dances in the air
In love's embrace, sweet peace will rise
Like enchanted whispers beneath open skies

In murmured streams and meadows wide
Love's gentle touch—a soothing tide
In every bloom, in every lease
In love's embrace, hearts find their peace

No tumult here, no strife, no bitter sting
Just melodies of joy, where bliss takes wing
In nature's arms, passion's solace we release
In love's own rhythm, we find lasting peace

So let us wander, hand in hand
Through meadows green and over shifting sand
In love's tranquil hues, all troubles cease
For only in its depths, we find eternal peace.

I am not sure how to introduce this next project. This one came to me while I was chatting to a close friend who had recently lost his wife. He is a great fan of the blues—artists like BB King, Gary Moore, etc. When he mentioned he still had the blues for his wife, it gave me the idea for this next poem: *I Still Got the Blues*.

# I Still Got the Blues

In midnight's embrace, where shadows dance
Whispers of memories—a bittersweet trance
A heart's lament, like a mournful hue
In every note, I still got the blues for you

Echoes of laughter, now distant and faint
In the soul's silent chambers, they endlessly paint
Yet amidst the tears and the moments we knew
In the quiet of the night, I still got the blues for you

The stars may shimmer, the world may spin
But in this heart of mine, you eternally begin
For love's melody forever rings true
In every beat, I still got the blues for you.

Sometimes, autism has a habit of trying to remind me that it's in control when I least expect it—before my new coping mechanisms kick in and get me back on track. But sometimes, I am a little slow to respond. This was written on one of those occasions: *Am I Lost*.

# Am I Lost

Have I lost who I am
To the shadows in the night?
Seeking truths in the dim
Lost dreams out of sight

Yet in whispers, faint and low
I hear echoes of my name
In the depths where doubts grow
I can and will find myself again

Through the maze of doubt and fear
I'll reclaim what's mine—I will rise
For within, my essence clear
Shines a light that never dies.

This next collection starts with a poem I wrote for an old blind man I used to meet when I worked in London. He was a lovely man who used to walk past my office with his gorgeous guide dog. I used to pop out, have chat with him, and cuddle his dog. Anyway, this is a short little ode to Bob (name changed).

# The Old Blind Man

In the place where light fears to tread
A blind man walks with footsteps bold
His world is shaped by whispers softly said
As darkness weaves stories yet untold

Through his fingertips, he reads the silent air
The winds carve a story on his old, weathered face
A world unseen, yet bringing mysteries to bare
As in his heart, every vision has its place

No gaze to capture colours bright and gold
Yet in his mind, a canvas painted so true
A symphony of sound, with imaginations to hold
Each step a dance, a rhythm born anew

This old blind man, with eyes kind and wise
Your soul like a beacon, lighting the darkest skies.

Keeping with the same theme, this is another short poem—this time for a deaf lady I knew when I was growing up. I was young when my mother introduced me to her. She was a friend of my mum's, and I remember being totally fascinated by how she interacted with the world around her. I used to write little messages to her, which she would read and then write back to me—I loved it. Anyway, this is a little ode to that lovely, kind lady: *The Deaf Lady*.

# The Deaf Lady

In a silent world, where echoes fail to ring
A deaf lady wanders, untouched by melodic spring
No orchestra of sound, no lyrics grace
Yet, in her heart, a vibrant world takes place

With no crashing waves or birds in song
In her silence, a rhyme so rare and strong
The dancing of hands, expressing tales to be told
In these quiet gestures, stories begin to unfold

She feels the pulse of life beneath her feet
Through silence, her world feels happy, complete
Rhythms dance within her busy mind
In quietude, her eyes informed—a wisdom refined

This deaf lady, living within silence so profound
Yet, in her world, a quiet beauty will always resound.

When I was young, I sometimes used to go and stay with my Nan and Grandad in Fulham, West London. On weekends, they used to take me to a market on North End Road. There was an old lady who always walked around the market wearing a red shawl. She fired my imagination, and thus, the following was born: *The Old Lady in the Marketplace.*

# The Old Lady in the Marketplace

In the marketplace, she stands each day
Wearing an old red shawl as she gently sways
With a stooped walk and knowing eyes
She weaves her stories, old and wise

Her face—a map of years gone by
Of laughter, loss, and long-gone sighs
With a basket full of herbs and spice
She shares her world with calm advice

Her voice—a gentle, soothing tone
In her world that no one else has known
The secrets of her heart, she rarely gives
In her lonely life, her sacred spirit lives

Beneath the sky's vast, changing hue
She stands—constant, tired, yet true
This old woman in the market square
This timeless soul, roaming without a care.

I was walking around an art gallery not so long ago when I saw a painting by an unknown artist. I really should have taken their name, but I didn't. Anyway, it was a gorgeous painting of a young girl—I would say an early teenager—sitting on a balcony in some Mediterranean country, looking very melancholy as she stared longingly at an imaginary distant horizon. When I got home, I put pen to paper, and the following poem materialised: *The Girl on the Balcony.*

# The Girl on the Balcony

She sat on the balcony, in melancholy's embrace
Soft whispers of twilight painting her face
Dreams danced in her eyes, in a dreamy light
Lost in the moment, in the satin hues of night

With a sigh, she pondered mysteries untold
In the hush of solitude, her thoughts gently unfold
Within the nigh of starlight, tales to be spun
In her soft, seductive world, where fantasies run

The night held her tight—a close, tender friend
As melodies began to sing an enchanting blend
On the balcony, she lingered, lost in reverie
Another dreamer in the night, struggling to be free.

Truthfully, I cannot remember how this poem came into existence. I found it among some older poems I have written through the years. But as I feel it has a significance to the softness a woman's love and tenderness can bring, I thought I would include it: *In a Woman's Tear.*

# In a Woman's Tear

In every tear that falls from a tender eye
Is a silent tale of love's profound embrace
For in those drops, emotions softly lie
As a woman's heart reveals its sacred space

Each tear, a jewel of her deepest care
Reflecting joys and sorrows entwined
Her love—a beacon shinning pure and rare
In moments where her soul is unconfined

Through tears of pain or happiness bright
She speaks a language word cannot convey
A testament to love's enduring light
That guides her through each night and every day

So, treasure tears that from her heart appear
For in their sacred flow, her love is crystal clear.

Bringing me to a poem I wrote for an organisation I work for, which wanted a poem to celebrate International Women's Day. With honour, I came up with the following: *International Women's Day.*

# International Women's Day

From ancient times to modern days
Women have shaped the world in countless ways
With wisdom's touch and courage's flame
They have kindled hope and fought for change

In tenderness and grace, women find their plight
In compassion, their empathy shines bold and bright
With every tear hides a strength unveiled
In every storm, their courage hailed

In nurturing love, they find their might
Their gentle touch healing every blight
Yet, in their eyes, a fire burns
To heal the past so the world can learn

A power coursing through veins of steel
In every heartbeat, an ancient reel
It dwells within a woman's tender gaze—
A resilience that heals in myriad ways

They dance with stars as they walk on air
Painting the sky with colours so rare
Their laughter echoing throughout the night
Dispelling the darkness with eternal light

In every woman, a universe resides
Where galaxies of dreams and hopes collide
Held within a woman's warm embrace
Is a fortitude that forever has its place.

Keeping on the theme of women, my mother has become very old and has dementia and other issues related to this horrible condition. After fighting with the local council for my mother's care, it became apparent that, my mother, like most older people in this country, is just a statistic—a number on someone's spreadsheet: *Is My Mother Now Just a Statistic?*

# Is My Mother Now Just a Statistic?

My mother is just a statistic on a spreadsheet
Lost in the sea of algorithms and charts
A number, a data point, a cell on a screen—
Her life reduced to a line on a list unseen

Her story, her struggles, her laughter, her pain—
Condensed to a figure, devoid of her name
No voice in the columns, no face in the rows
Just a fraction, a fragment, where ink stains grow

The warmth of her touch, the light in her eyes
Now invisible to those who simply analyses
The tears she shed, the dreams she chased
Erased in the formulas, gone without trace

A pivot table can't capture her grace
A graph cannot chart the lines on her face
Her essence, her spirit, her love, her strife—
Vanished in numbers, stripped of her life

But behind every digit, there's a pulse, a breath—
A mother, a wife, facing life and death
In the heart of data, a human resides
With a life being lived—spreadsheets cannot hide

So, when you see her as just a statistical spot
Remember, my mother is someone, not just a dot
Her legacy lives beyond a PowerPoint view
And is still cherished by those who love her so true.

So, what if love became extinct? If we all became numbers on a spreadsheet, what would we be then? What If love Became Extinct?

# What If Love Became Extinct?

In a world where love is no more
Were echoes of laughter fade to lore
Cold winds blow through hollow hearts
A shadowed earth where joy departs

Once vibrant hues now turn to grey
Sunset's warmth has slipped away
As silent whispers fill the air
A vacant stare, a voided care.

What if love's light ceased to shine
Leaving darkness so divine?
Empty souls, a barren ground
In loveless silence, we are bound

Yet, in the shadows, hope would gleam—
A distant, softly spoken dream
For love, though gone, can never die
It lives forever in memory's gentle sigh.

As a little bonus, now let's step into a world where logic takes a holiday and whimsy reigns supreme! I am thrilled to present "A Handful of Nonsense Poems," a delightful collection that dances on the edge of reason and celebrates the joy of the absurd.

In the following pages, you'll find poems that twist reality into giggles and turn everyday moments into fantastical adventures. From playful puns and peculiar predicaments to oddball questions and curious conundrums, each poem is a playful romp through the land of imagination.

So, prepare to let go of the ordinary and dive headfirst into a realm where the moon might just be made of cheese, where trains run perfectly on time—or maybe not! Whether you're young or simply young at heart, these nonsensical verses are sure to tickle your funny bone and spark a twinkle in your eye.

Join me on this whimsical journey, where sense is optional and fun is guaranteed. After all, in a world of nonsense, anything is possible!

# A Whisky Whimsy

Oh, the whisky wobbles on the shelf
Dancing like a mischievous elf
With a clink and a clatter, it sings a tune—
A melody supplied by a tipsy moon

"Cheers!" cried the bottle, a merry toast
To the phantom that loves to boast
In the barrel-aged forest where spirits grow
The oaken trees sway to and fro

With a hip and a hiccup, the bottle spoke
Telling tales of the smoky oak
It whispered secrets of peat and spice
Of pirates and dragons and sugar mice

The ice cubes giggled as they danced a jig
In a tumbler as big as a fig
The whisky laughed with a golden glow
As two bubbles rose from the depths below

Oh, the whisky waltzed with a tonic's cheer
In a boozy ballet, without a fear
They stumbled and fumbled on the tip of a tongue—
With a slosh and a dash, the song was sung

So, raise your glass to the brew
To the whisky whimsy, the spirit stew
For in every drop, a tale unfolds—
A barrel of laughter, a dram of gold.

# The Little Girl and the Ghost

In a house with crooked halls
Lived a girl with tiny dolls
Her hair, like spun gold in the sun
She played all day and had such fun

One night, she heard a gentle "Boo!"
A friendly ghost, all dressed in blue
He floated in with a wispy grin
His see-through face as pale as gin

"Hello there, girl!" the ghost did say
"Do you want to have some fun and play?"
He twirled around, a spectral sprite
And filled the room with glowing light

She giggled at his ghostly charms
As he drifted near with open arms
They danced atop the creaky floors
Through secret walls and hidden doors

They flew through kitchens, past the clocks
Sipped phantom tea, munched shadow rocks
The ghost told tales of times long gone
Of knights and dragons and a haunted prawn

The little girl, with eyes so wide
Laughed and laughed until she cried
"You're the funniest ghost I've ever seen!"
She said while dressed in a spectral sheen

The ghost just winked and spun around
A ghostly giggle, a joyful sound
He puffed his cheeks and tried to sneeze
But only managed a spooky wheeze

When dawn approached, the ghost turned pale
He floated up, a misty trail
"It's time for me to disappear,"
He whispered softly in her ear

"But I'll be back, you wait and see
For another night of ghostly glee!"
The girl waved bye with a cheerful shout
As the ghostly form just faded out

In the house with crooked halls
She'd play again with her tiny dolls
But she kept an eye on the darkened night
For her friend, the ghost, with a smile so light

And so, they say, if you listen close
You'll hear the laughter of a little girl and a ghost
In a house where whimsy never sleeps
Where secrets and friendship run ever so deep.

# What If the Moon Was Made Out of Cheese?

Is the moon made of cheese? Oh, what a thought!
A round, glowing ball of dairy—not naught
Is it cheddar, or Swiss with holes so bright
Or maybe it's Brie, glowing soft in the night?

The astronauts went with a big silver spoon
To scoop up a bite from the bright, cheesy moon
They brought back a wedge to nibble and munch
And declared, "It's a cracker's dream for lunch!"

In the sky hangs a wheel of creamy delight
Orbiting Earth in the starry night
Is it sharp like a Gouda, or mild as can be?
Perhaps it's a blend of Camembert and Brie?

The ringed cheese moon has a rind so green—
It's the finest fromage you've ever seen
With a sprinkle of stardust and a dash of delight
It's the perfect treat on a lunar night.

So, if you look up at the night sky so high,
And see the full moon with a glimmering eye
Just think of the cheeses, so melty and round
And know that in any imagination, a story is found.

For who can say if it's true or it's a tease?
Is the moon made of rocks, or maybe… just cheese?

# The Winemaker
# and His Trusty Barrel

In a cellar, where shadows play
Lived a winemaker, old and a little grey
With a twinkle in his eye and a grape-stained nose
He whispers secrets only the vineyard knows

His trusty companion, a barrel so round
Stood stout and silent, without a sound
The barrel was grand, with a belly so wide
It could hold all the stars if the stars could hide

"Ah, my dear barrel," the winemaker mused
"You hold the finest drink, so carefully infused
With whispers of oak and a kiss from the vine
Together we make the most magical wine."

The barrel creaked with an ancient groan
As if to say, "I hold the essence of stone
The laughter of leaves, the warmth of the sun
In my wooden heart, all flavours become one."

One night, the winemaker, in a fanciful spree
Decided to make a wine as wild as the sea
He tossed in some moonbeams, a handful of stars
A sprinkle of comets from distant quasars

He added a splash of rainbow's hue
A pinch of twilight, a dawn's fresh dew
He stirred it with the wind's gentle breeze
And seasoned it well with a little sneeze

The barrel bubbled with a gurgling laugh
As the wine took on a scent of myth and a dash of half
"Cheers to the wonder!" the winemaker cried
As the barrel burped, trying to remain quite dignified

He bottled the blend with labels of gold
"Stardust & Grape, A Tale Untold."
The corks popped off with a magical fizz
Revealing a wine that simply is

The townsfolk gathered to taste this delight
And found themselves floating, as light as a kite
Each sip, they soared on clouds of cream
Lost in a most whimsical dream

The winemaker grinned, his work was done
His barrel, now empty, sighed, "That was fun!"
They sat in the cellar, content and proud
As the townsfolk danced on the Milky Way's cloud.

# Ode to Tea

Oh, noble brew, thy essence pure
In porcelain cups, thou dost allure
With a fragrant steam, a gentle lure
Thy glorious tea, forever endure

From distant lands, thy leaves unfurl
In gardens green, where breezes swirl
With tender care, they're plucked a pearl
To grace our cups, a gift to the world

In a morning's hush, this art the balm
A sip of solace, a healing calm
Through whispered mist, we find our psalm
In thy embrace, all troubles disarm

With jasmine's kiss or early grey's sigh
Or chai's embrace, beneath India's sky
In every sip, a melody lies
A symphony of taste, none can deny

Oh, tea, thou bring a timeless art
A ritual cherished, never to depart
In ode to thee, eternal friend
Tea, a joy that knows no end.

# What If Trains Ran on Time?

What if trains ran on time? It would surly cause a scene!
The world would be tidy, precise, and rather pristine
The clocks would all chime with a harmonious clatter
And schedules would dance in a punctual matter

The stations would hum with a rhythmic beat
As conductors tap-danced on their swift-moving feet
Passengers would hop like popcorn in glee
"On time, on time! Just as it should be!"

The platforms would glow with a gleaming light
With not a single slow train or delay in sight
No more mad dashes or frantic rush
Just calm, serene, and orderly hush

The trains would all whistle in perfect pitch
With gears that clicked without a hitch
The tracks would stretch like a well-pressed seam
In a world where being late is just a bad dream

Imagine the chaos of everything right
No lost luggage, or no missed flight!
No excuses, "The train was late!"
Just perfect timing at every gate

But what of the thrill of the unexpected delay
The stories shared along the way?
The friendships formed in the waiting line
All those moments, which are surely divine

Would life lose its zest, its unexpected grace
Without those moments, a slower pace?
Would we miss the charm of a serendipitous glitch
In a world too smooth, without a hitch?

So, what if trains ran on time every day?
Perhaps we'd find it all a bit grey
For the world loves its quirks, its mishaps and turns
Where the wheels sometimes wobble and the engine burns

So, let's embrace the delays, the wait, the surprise
For they bring colour to the routine in disguise
A world too perfect would surely feel flat
So, here's to the late train, and that… is simply that!

# Can I Really 'Catch' a Cold?

Can I catch a cold like catching a ball
With a net, a glove, or a hat that's tall?
Is it a slippery fish in a frosty stream
Or a runaway kite on a chilly dream?

Do colds hide in corners, waiting to leap
Like sneaky ninjas who never sleep?
Do they sneak in with a tickly sneeze
Or float on the breeze like autumn leaves?

Can I trap a cold in a butterfly net
Or catch it by chasing a snowy sunset?
Do colds hang out on icicle trees
Whispering, "Boo!" in the cool night breeze?

Perhaps they're like marbles, rolling along
Bumping and clinking in a wintery song
Or maybe they're stars in a snowy sky
That twinkle and sparkle, then say goodbye

Can I catch a cold in a biscuit jar
With a snap of the lid, like a shooting star?
Or maybe in mittens, snug and tight
Catching a chill in the cold moonlight?

But wait! Can I really "catch" a cold
Like a runaway puppy, big and bold?
Or is it just a silly turn of phrase
Like catching shadows on misty days?

So, if I catch a cold, will it sing a song
Or dance a jig all night long?
Or will it simply come and simply go
Like a frosty breath in a morning glow?

Oh, catching a cold is such a funny thing
Like catching raindrops in a fairy's wing
It's nonsense, really, don't you see?
It's just a silly trick of the mind… Maybe.

# Time, What Time?

What is time? A wiggly worm
A clock that likes to twist and turn
A backward running, upside-down
A tick-tock hat, a cuckoo crown

Is time a soul that's never hot
A pot of stew that's lost the plot?
A melting clock upon the wall
A noodle that's too long and far too tall?

Is time a race with no finish line
A wibbly-wobbly ball of twine?
A slippery fish in a fancy suit
A flute that plays without a toot?

Does time come in a bottle blue
With bubbles and a fizzy hue?
Or is it liking a sneaky little sprite
That hides away from morning light?

Perhaps it's just a dance we do
A jig that makes our feet go woo
A game we play with twisty rules
A splash of nonsense, a pool of fools

So, what is time? Oh, who can say
A riddle wrapped in a sunbeam's ray
A jester's laugh, a fleeting wink
A thought that's gone before you think

In the end, it's just a rhyme
A silly, man-made, hourly chime
A jumbled mixed-up sort of mime
Oh, who knows really, what is time?

# What Is Human-Kind?

What is human-kind, you ask with a grin
A tumble of thoughts, a jumble within?
Are we from a far-off cosmic star
Or moonbeams caught in an empty jar?

Are we like donuts, round and sweet
With sprinkles of kindness, a tasty treat?
Or are we like socks in a washing machine whirl
Mismatched and missing, caught in a twirl?

Are we puzzle pieces that never quite fit
Or silly stories, from a wobbly script?
Maybe we're ice cream, in a hundred flavours
A mixture of moods and curious capers

Perhaps we're balloons, high in the sky
Full of hot air with reasons to fly
Or could we be teacups, delicate and small
Filled with warm thoughts, or nothing at all?

Are we question marks in a book of facts
Or silly drops of water on rubbery ducks' backs?
Maybe we're gardens, wild and green
With flowers and weeds and everything between

Are we like bubbles, bright and thin
Popping with laughter or blowing in the wind?
Or maybe we're clocks, ticking away
Counting moments in a curious ballet

Could we be whispers in a thunderstorm
Or cuddly bears keeping hearts warm?
Are we like kites on a breezy day
Tangled in strings, fumbling our way?

So, what is human-kind, in truth or jest
A muddle, a mix, a wondrous quest?
We're dreams and doodles, odd and grand
A curious bunch in a mixed-up land

Human-kind, what a quirky find
A sprinkle of love, a mysterious mind
Simply putting up with daily grind
What a puzzle we are, this human-kind.

# The Old
# Book on the Shelf

In a dusty nook, on a creaky old shelf
Sat a forgotten book, all by itself
Its cover was faded, its pages were torn
A relic from times long past and forlorn

The books beside it whispered and gossiped
Tales of dragons and daring, oh, how they bopped
But the forgotten book just sat there in peace
Its stories locked up, in a quiet release

Once, it had glowed with bright words and cheer
With characters bold, it was quite the premier
But now it sat lonely, in a shadowy spot
In the land of the lost, a book quite forgot

"Who knows what's inside?" the big dictionary said
"Perhaps it's a story of butter and bread!"
"Or maybe of penguins who dance in the snow!
"Chimed in the atlas, "I'd like to know!"

The cookbooks imagined a recipe rare
For soup made of moonbeams or magical air
The fairy tales giggled, "It's probably full
Of knights and of fairies and a cranky old bull!"

But nobody read it, nobody knew
The secrets it held, the adventures, the blue
Its spine gave a creak, a sigh of regret
Yet it sat on the shelf, quiet and set

One day, a breeze blew in from the door
And the forgotten book fell to the floor
It opened up wide, with a dusty old sneeze
Pages fluttered and flapped like leaves in the breeze

Out came a dragon, with scales made of cheese
And a knight with a sword made of rainbows and peas
A princess who laughed with a nose that could sing
And a pirate who danced on a big bouncy spring

The books all around gasped in delight
As the forgotten book glowed, so vivid and bright
Its tales were alive, so wondrous and wild
With a wink and a bow, it laughed like a child

Then, just as quick as the magic appeared
The book closed shut; the room slightly cheered
Back to its spot on the shelf, it returned—
The forgotten book, with stories that burned

And there it sits still, in its dusty old nook
The forgotten treasure, the mysterious book
Its tales are untold, its wonders unseen
A whisper of magic in a shelf's quiet dream.

As you turn the final page of this collection, I hope these poems have been a journey through the myriad colours of life and imagination. From the whimsical to the profound, the light-hearted to the introspective, each verse has sought to capture a moment, a thought, or a feeling from my life's journey, and which I hope also resonates within you all.

In poetry, I think we find the freedom to explore the world not only as it is but as it could be—a place of endless possibilities, where words dance and emotions breathe. Through this book, I like to think you have traversed landscapes of the heart and mind, encountering both familiar comforts and delightful surprises.

As you close this book, remember that poetry doesn't end with the last line. It lives on in the spaces between words, in the quiet moments of reflection, and in the shared experiences that bring people and minds closer together. Let these poems be a spark—a reminder to find beauty in the everyday, to seek out wonder in the mundane, and to embrace the full spectrum of human experience.

Thank you for joining me on this poetic adventure. May these poems continue to inspire and accompany you, like an old friend, whenever you need a gentle reminder of the magic and mystery in the world. Until we meet again on another page, keep the verses alive in your heart and let your own words take flight.

**Thank you!**